STRATEGIC TALENT MANAGEMENT

How To Boost Your **Profits** In A Disruptive Economy

From The International Best Selling Author

Dr. Denis Cauvier

Other books by Dr. Denis Cauvier:

- How to Hire the Right Person
- How To Keep Your Staff Productive & Happy
- Achieve It! A Personal Success Journal
- The ABC's of Making Money (co-authored with Alan Lysaght)
- Attracting, Selecting and Retaining GREAT People
- The ABC's of Making Money 4 Teens (co-authored with Alan Lysaght)
- 101 Low Cost/High Impact Recruiting Methods
- Hired 2.0 Recruiting Exceptional Talent at the Speed of Light

First Edition, First Printing – Copyright © 2018 by DAX Enterprises International Inc.

Cover design and layout by Syed Muhammad Salman

Edited by Judi Blaze

Back cover photo by Martin Spicer

Printed in Canada by RR Donnelley Inc.

10 9 8 7 6 5 4 3 2 1

ISBN 978-0-9736514-7-8

Acknowledgements

This work, like all of my books, is a synergistic product of many minds. I have gained so many insights and gems of wisdom from numerous colleagues, thousands of clients, and countless attendees at my various presentations around the world. Some specific people I would like to acknowledge include:

- The late Og Mandino and Bill Gibson, my first business mentors, who shared so much with me during the critical early years.

- Syed Mohammed, for the book cover design and layout.

- Judi Blaze, for editing the manuscript.

- The awesome Educational team at YPO Global, by whom I have been honored to be selected as a Speaker Resource for YPO Global regions and chapters.

- My father, who is one of the most passionate cheerleaders of my efforts.

- My late mother, who has shown so much dignity, grace and mental toughness in the face of tremendous adversity.

- My two wonderful daughters, for bringing so much light into my life.

- Debbie, my life partner, for her un-wavering support and encouragement.

Table of Contents

Foreword

I have known Denis for many years and I am delighted he is leveraging his global experience as a professional speaker, international best-selling author, and turn around Talent Management/HR consultant to provide proven methods in which business owners, senior executives and Talent Management professionals can better position themselves to deliver the strategic solutions their organizations need to survive and thrive in a disruptive economy. In my experience, leading organizations are underpinned with strategic Talent Management investments that generate both short- and long-term return on investments. This investment focus requires all leaders and the teams that they lead to fully understand the organization's commercial and developmental needs.

Denis's book ***Strategic Talent Management – How to Boost Your Profits in a Disruptive Economy*** is full of proven, practical, and ready-to-use tools, templates, and checklists that will facilitate any organization's success. Companies that turn away from a long-term investment in Talent Management to satisfy short term financial needs ultimately fall out of the leading company category. If you want to succeed, Dr. Denis Cauvier's timely book shows you the way!

Peter Nixon, FCPA-CA, www.PotentialDialogue.com, Author of Dialogue Gap (Wiley, 2012), Negotiation (Wiley, 2005)

A Personal Note from the Author

The Young Presidents Organization (YPO) recently selected me as a Speaker Resource to showcase to their global network of over 400 chapters in 130 countries. YPO asked me this question, "Having shared your thought-provoking messages with over one million people in 50 countries, what have you discovered is a common trend throughout the world of Talent Management?"

My response is as follows: *"I would categorize this common trend as a missed opportunity. Too many organizations view Talent Management/HR as a 'Cost Center'. For over 30 years, I have advocated that HR needs to be seen and held accountable as a 'Profit Center.' Today's hyper competitive and disruptive business environment requires an agile workforce to survive let alone succeed. To accomplish this we need to change our focus from **spending** money on Talent Management and instead start making strategic **investments**. When we think in terms of investments, we expect certain returns from these investments. Talent Management is no different. Each investment needs to be analyzed to consider the business case rationale before proceeding, and then measured to determine the actual contribution made to the bottom line."*

One of my greatest sources of professional pride is my track record in helping companies reframe their perspective on Talent Management/ HR, by creating specific strategies to maximize their returns on all HR investments. These investments can reduce the time and cost of hiring, increase levels of productivity, reduce employee turnover, enhance customer satisfaction, improve sales, and boost profits. This book is the result of several decades of research into the best Talent Management practices. It is the product of over 30 years of experience as a professional speaker/trainer and consultant. Although the bulk of the book deals with lessons learned through direct experience, a great deal of what I know today was gleaned from relentless self-education, leading countless seminars and workshops, and making use of the best ideas I have been exposed to over the years.

Although I have made considerable effort to indicate the source of any words that are not mine, I may have inadvertently failed to acknowledge the original source in some instances. If this has happened, I would be pleased to receive any information that helps me to properly acknowledge my sources.

I sincerely hope you will be inspired to use this book as a constant source of practical information, to ensure that you enjoy a fantastic rate of return on your Talent Management investments!

Best wishes,
Dr. Denis Cauvier

Chapter One:
Talent Management Boosting Profits

> **There are two types of people in the business community: those who produce results and those who give you reasons why they didn't.**
>
> Peter Drucker

DID YOU KNOW

Executive Insomnia

According to Forbes Magazine the following are the top concerns of senior executives in order of frequency.

- Attraction/Engagement/Retention of talent
- Profits/Cash-Flow
- Brand Reputation
- Competition
- Geo Political Changes
- Economy
- Regulatory Changes
- Commodity/Currency Changes

Strategic Talent Management

Even though it is increasingly difficult to predict the future, it is still essential to identify and understand the basic social, economic and technological trends that will affect businesses in the next ten years. The digital age has ushered in The Disruptive Economy — an economic environment that is fast, open, and challenging. These changes have directly impacted traditional industries, which have subsequently vanished or been greatly transformed. If organizations want to succeed in these turbulent times, they must learn how to ride the waves of change — the good, the bad, and the sometimes terrifying. The most important key to surviving and prospering during times of uncertainty is to tap into the potential of your human capital.

Over the past 30 years I have worked closely with thousands of CEO's, Presidents, and Managing Directors of very successful organizations all over the world. These people range in age from their mid twenties to their late seventies, and are drawn from all major cultures and religions, including those who identify themselves as atheists or agnostics. All of these people share one common trait: they invest a minimum of one third to one half of their time focusing on Talent Management issues. They have correctly determined that it is not so much their product, services IP or location that provides their biggest strategic advantage as it is the possession of an agile team of highly engaged and competent people. Strategic talent makes all of the difference.

In my experience, the best way to act on this insight is to immediately change the antiquated notion of spending money on staff to a perspective from which the HR function is seen as a profit center requiring strategic investments.

Strategic Talent Management

DID YOU KNOW

70% of CEOs cite human capital as the single biggest contributor to sustained economic value. - **Global IBM Study**

71% of CEOs ranked employee engagement as a top driver to achieving success. – **Harvard Business Review**

⚠ Danger

SME's Top 10 Labor Challenges:

1. Attracting qualified candidates
2. Retaining key employees
3. Lack of leadership capacity
4. Engaging workforce
5. Lack of succession plan
6. Employee competencies not aligned with organisational priorities
7. Modifying work arrangements to meet labour regulations
8. Developing skills fast enough to meet opportunities
9. Lack of collaboration
10. Lack of "diversity connection" internal/external to organization

Strategic Talent Management

"Talent Management" and "Agility"

Talent Management (TM) and Agility have become buzzwords that are perhaps overused in business today. Before proceeding, it makes sense to share my perspective on these two concepts.

First, what is TM? Although there are many definitions, in the simplest terms, TM is the recruitment, engagement, development, promotion, and retention of people who can contribute to an organization's objectives. Effective TM systems build profitable companies by ensuring that key people have the core competencies and attitudes needed to realize the corporate vision strategy.

Agile, nimble, resilient—these words describe the people most companies want to hire, retain, and develop. They describe the ideal workforce that will thrive in the disruptive economy. An agile or change-ready organization is able to adapt quickly to changing circumstances; it is ready for anything. It can respond instantaneously to changing customer demands. The agile organization innovates rapidly and immediately tailors products and services to customer needs.

DID YOU KNOW

In a business sense, the term "agile" originated in 2001 in the course of discussions among a small group of IT leaders. It refers to an approach to software development. The "Agile Manifesto" laid out the following 12 principles:

1. Our highest priority is to satisfy the customer through early and continuous delivery of valuable software.

2. Welcome changing requirements, even late in development. Agile processes harness change for the customer's competitive advantage.

3. Deliver working software frequently, from a couple of weeks to a couple of months, with a preference for shorter timescales.

4. Business people and developers must work together daily throughout the project.

5. Build projects around motivated individuals. Give them the environment and support they need, and trust them to get the job done.

6. The most efficient and effective method of conveying information to and within a development team is face-to-face conversation.

7. Working software is the primary measure of progress.

8. Agile processes promote sustainable development. The sponsors, developers, and users should be able to maintain a constant pace indefinitely.

9. Continuous attention to technical excellence and good design enhances agility.

10. Simplicity—the art of maximizing the amount of work not done—is essential.

11. The best architectures, requirements, and designs emerge from self-organizing teams.

12. At regular intervals, the team reflects on how to become more effective, then tunes and adjusts its behavior accordingly.

Source: **Agile Alliance**

 **Danger**

Consider for a moment that 50 to 60% of most companies' operating expenses are workforce costs. Take another moment to think about this:

- "50% of the average company's workforce capacity is wasted on non-productive efforts."—Corporate Strategy Board, Measuring What Matters

- "84% of companies are not using their workforce to its full potential." —Saratoga Institute

- "95% of the workforce does not understand its employer's strategy and goals." —Norton and Kaplan

These numbers clearly indicate that there are huge bottom-line gains to be had by fully tapping into a company's human resource capital. I contend that the best way to begin making use of this resource is to immediately start treating HR as a profit center.

According to U.S. government statistics, there are 76 million baby boomers in America alone who are due to retire within the next decade. The beleaguered world economy is putting unusual pressures on organizations, requiring them to do much more with a lot less. In the marketplace, there is a shortage of high performers in the marketplace. Approximately

Strategic Talent Management

70% of clients say it is hard to find high performers, and almost as many say it is hard to retain high performers once they are found. Moreover, companies are seeing a tremendous increase in turnover, partly because millennial employees are more inclined to change jobs and careers to fulfill their personal needs and goals. [Note: I will cover the management of millennials, and the other three-workplace demographic groups, at the beginning of Chapter four].

The bottom line in today's disruptive economy is that organizations must focus squarely on talent; on finding it, nurturing it, exploiting it, and retaining it.

How can wise TM investments boost profits?

Your organization can significantly boost its financial success by making wise HR investments. The following research shows how effective TM programs and practices impact the bottom line.

- **High-performing TM practices and outcomes.** An Academy of Management Journal study of 1,000 publicly held U.S. firms found that a 10% increase in funds allocated to effective TM practices resulted in:
    - an increase of $27,044 in sales per employee,
    - an increase of $18,641 in market value per employee, and
    - a 7.05% decrease in employee turnover.

- **TM best practices and market value.** In a longitudinal study of 750 large North American and European companies by Watson Wyatt Worldwide, improving key human capital practices led to an increase of 47% in market value. The human capital practices that were improved in this study included total rewards and accountability, a collegial and flexible workplace, recruiting and retention excellence, communications integrity, and focused TM service technologies.

Strategic Talent Management

- **TM best practices and market perceptions.** In a study of 590 companies by Delaney & Huselid, it was found that progressive TM practices (including selective staffing, training, and incentive compensation) were strongly related to the company being perceived internally and externally as an employer of choice in their marketplace.

- **TM contributes to engagement and safety.** A large manufacturing company saved $1,721,760 in safety costs by increasing employee engagement. They found that engaged employees are five times less likely to have accidents, and that the average cost of an accident for engaged employees was $329 less than for non-engaged employees.

- **TM driving engagement and profit.** A large-scale study by ISR found that companies with high levels of employee engagement realized a 15% increase in net profit, compared to companies with low engagement.

High Performers Drive Profit

The McKinsey Quarterly surveyed 410 corporate officers at 35 large U.S. companies, and reported that high performing employees generated:

- 40% more productivity in operational roles,
- 49% more profit in general management roles, and
- 67% more revenue in sales roles.

Talent Boosts Productivity

The Journal of Applied Psychology investigated the economic value added as a result of TM programs. It found that superior workers are 148% more productive than average workers. In other words, a superior worker with a $100,000 salary produces about $148,000 of work, while a poor performer has a production value of only $52,000.

Strategic Talent Management

Executive Talent Impacts Profits

According to research conducted by R.J. Vance, choosing executives with the requisite skills and knowledge for their position is worth $3 million in profit per executive.

Engaged Workers Stay and Produce

As reported in HR Magazine, one large software company found that highly engaged employees are 3.3 times more likely to be top performers, and 5 times less likely to voluntarily leave the company. The study also found that sales people who are fully committed to their job and company, outperform disengaged sales people by 82%.

DID YOU KNOW

How much of a difference can one top performing employee make?

Dr. John Sullivan of San Francisco State University estimated the differential revenue production between an average employee and a top performer with the same job description as follows:

- top performer 10 times the average employee at Netflix
- top performer 25 times the average employee at Apple
- top performer 100+ times the average employee at Google

> **The leader is the servant who removes the obstacles that prevent people from doing their jobs.**
>
> Max Depree

Something worth considering

What would you do if you found a TM leader who could improve your company's profit margins, reduce the cost of goods sold, increase sales, and increase the price/earnings ratio? while reducing overhead costs to the business — and still deliver traditional HR services?

Most CEOs would react in two ways:

- Why is this individual wasting their time in an HR department?
- Why don't I get this level of HR performance?

I have been an advocate of the concept of HR as a profit center for more than three decades. Happily, this notion is gaining popularity. Professor David Ulrich of the University of Michigan, a leading expert on HR competency models, sees the changing business world as a 20/20/60 proposition. Of executives surveyed, attitudes toward HR were distributed as follows:

- 20% believed that the HR department should remain as administrative overhead and only perform transactional work.
- 20% currently use the HR department as an active and innovative business solution partner.
- 60% are starting to expect the HR department to partner with other departments to improve the company's core competencies and competitive advantages. (Happily, more HR people are stepping up to the plate and delivering the goods).

Strategic Talent Management

What is driving this thinking? The short answer is: competitive pressure in a disruptive business world — competitive pressure for sales, talent, and profits. Most CEOs (and their CFOs) are held accountable for three general, but powerful, results: increasing revenue, generating cash, and reducing costs. In order to focus on these three priorities and grow their businesses, executives are dropping old ways of thinking that no longer work.

The view of the HR department strictly as a cost center is one of the paradigms needing replacement. Such transactional HR activities as payroll, benefits administration, and records keeping can easily be outsourced or digitized with significant cost savings.

For many CEOs, viewing the TM function as a profit center takes getting used to. "That's not the way things have been," they say. Then they ask themselves these key questions:

- What's in it for my company?
- How will this improve our level of agility?
- How does this get us new customers and retain our current customers?
- Where is the improvement in revenue and profits?
- Where is the proof of ROI?

Once they get solid answers to these questions from competent, profit-oriented TM leaders, these same CEOs are quick to change their thinking. Over the past decade, CEOs began demanding that their HR functions become knowledgeable partners with all other disciplines to advance the business plan of the company. Individual functional silos are counterproductive. Finance, sales, marketing, operations, and TM should no longer exist as standalone entities; they need to become inter-dependent and interactive.

Change Your Expectations of the HR Function

How can you begin to shift your thinking about the HR function in your organization? Consider these three emerging concepts in the practice of TM:

Strategic Talent Management

1. **What value does the TM function bring to your organization?**
   Many HR teams lack a vision that includes their value to their organization:
   - Do TM activities directly help your company achieve its broad business objectives?
   - Are TM investments based on business case analyses?
   - Are TM solutions measured in terms of ROI?

2. **What value does the TM function generate for your customers?**
   Customers are the end users of your company's product or service. Sales and quality are no longer the exclusive domain of the sales and quality assurance teams. Edwards Deming taught organizations that quality and value must be built into every step of the process. TM leaders shouldn't just hire a salesperson based on a manager's request. The end result of TM's recruiting and hiring efforts should be a customer who interacts with a new salesperson in the course of receiving world-class service from the company. TM then plays a role in ensuring that the company is (or becomes) the vendor of choice for that customer.

3. **What are the prerequisite core competencies of TM leaders who are credible strategic partners with the rest of the executive team?** Each company and industry should generate its own list of core business skills that TM teams must have (that go beyond the traditional transactional HR skills).

Remember, the biggest barrier to profitability is ignorance. Your employees must know how your company makes money, how it achieves its objectives, and how all of the various functions interact. The notion that only finance people need to know about finance, or that marketing people are the only people who need to know about marketing is simply wrong. In today's business environment, profitable organizations need highly skilled employees who can solve complex problems using a multi-disciplinary approach.

Strategic Talent Management

How to Turn TM into a Profit Center

So how can your company make the transition to profitable TM? Here are several suggestions, all based on the belief that the more your employees become aware and accountable for their contributions to the bottom line, the better your company will perform.

- **Implement a leadership development program.** This program should include hands-on training in all of the functional disciplines.

- **Insist that TM staff receive financial training.** Financial training is necessary if TM staff is to be able to understand the impact of cash flow, receivables, billing cycles, and so forth. If you're a public company, teach TM staff to understand your company's annual report.

- **Have TM staff participate in sales strategies, customer visits, and technology reviews.** Encourage them to learn quality methods, to process improvement techniques, terms and conditions, and to engage in contract negotiations with suppliers and customers. Use your TM staff as process consultants, and train them so they can assist with growth initiatives.

- **Most importantly, hold all employees accountable for achieving the "critical numbers" established for your company.**

Treat your TM leaders as a full business partners. They will rise to the occasion and surprise you by building your bottom line and becoming a profit center contributor, while simultaneously discharging their traditional responsibilities. Treating TM leaders as full partners will allow them to become more proficient at both their expanded and traditional roles. In the intense and brutally competitive business environment of our global and digital world, everyone in your company must contribute to the fullest extent of his or her ability.

Strategic Talent Management

Focus on Revenue and Profit Growth, not Cost Containment

For the past few decades, the human resource function has myopically focused on process efficiency. Much of this misguided focus is attributable to pressure from the finance function and the budgeting process. This pressure can be relaxed by proactively developing the business case for all activities undertaken in TM.

Unfortunately, a business case is rarely developed, and the HR function continues to make trade-offs between quality and cost. This never-ending focus, while easy to accomplish and attractive to some, fails to address critical business problems that could be resolved with real TM solutions. Cost containment is comparable to periodically replacing water-stained acoustic ceiling tiles instead of calling in a roofer to fix the root problem. Replacing the tiles indefinitely is much more expensive than fixing the leak once and for all.

Proving the Productivity, Revenue and Profit Impact of TM

It's not enough to believe that TM activities and programs actually work. You must also be able to prove that they positively impact employee productivity, revenue, and profit. Unfortunately, most HR professionals go about proving that impact the wrong way. The process of demonstrating business impact should start by assessing all current TM programs to establish a baseline for future analysis. Once you have caught up, step two is to keep current by evaluating all newly proposed programs using the same process.

Strategic Talent Management

Key Talent Management Metrics

DID YOU KNOW

The Society of Human Resources Management has determined that the following TM Metrics are being used by their member organizations.

- 62% Employee turnover rate
- 50% Health care cost per employee
- 46% Time to hire
- 38% Cost per hire
- 37% Workers compensation per employee
- 35% Absenteeism rate
- 32% Worker's compensation incident rate
- 28% Employee productivity
- 27% Employee turnover costs
- 22% Prorated merit increases
- 21% HR department budget per full time employee
- 18% Cost of labour per location/ geographic region
- 18% Vacancy rate
- 18% Revenue per employee
- 15% Training ROI
- 8% HR/TM ROI

Strategic Talent Management

> **The continued survival of the organization depends on having the right people in the right places at the right time.**
>
> Peter Drucker

According to The Saratoga Institute, labor costs account for between 40 to 60% of most companies' operating expenses. So a great starting point is to examine the cost of staff turnover and how it affects the bottom line. Below is a simple, straightforward tool to help you begin the process of determining the actual costs involved with staff turnover. This chart is a starting point only; the process can and should become more detailed, to generate much more specific answers.

As a consultant, I work with many companies, and part of what I deliver is customized, software-based employee-turnover cost calculators. These plug-in-the-numbers tools quickly and accurately generate cost estimates as well as identifying specific problem areas. Readers interested in exploring these types of consulting solutions are encouraged to contact me directly at www.deniscauvier.com.

Strategic Talent Management

What is the Cost of Staff Turnover?

Table 1 shows the layout of a tool to estimate the cost of staff turnover.

Actual Cost to Hire One Person	Number Hours	Hourly Rate	Total Cost
Recruiting, Selection & Hiring Costs			
Salaries and other benefits of staff involved in hiring process			
Third-party recruitment fees			
Employee referral bonus			
Design and running of job ad			
Correspondence, telephone calls, fax transmissions, travel expenses of recruitment, medical exam costs, company literature, selection tests			
Reference checks			
Negotiating & finalizing employee contract			
Cost of relocating new employee			
Signing bonus			
Orientation and Training Costs			
Orientation (new hire processing, orientation materials and briefing)			
Uniforms & equipment issued			
Training (in-house training/coaching, training materials, external training)			
Performance assessment costs			
(A) Total Actual Costs to Hire One Person			

Cost of Hiring the Wrong Person	$ Costs
Termination (processing, exit interviews, severance and/or legal)	
Loss of productivity of employee, co-workers or supervisor prior to departure	
Loss of productivity of co-workers or supervisor during vacancy	
Loss of productivity of co-workers or supervisor during orientation & training	
Loss of productivity of new hire during transition period	
Increased defects/operating errors during vacancy	
Dissatisfied or lost clients	
Misused material or damaged equipment	
Decrease in morale due to high turnover	
(B) Total Cost of Hiring the Wrong Person	$
(C) Total Cost of One Employee Turnover (A + B = C)	$

The PROFIT Model for Maximizing ROI in TM

Many years ago, I created "The PROFIT Model for Maximizing ROI in TM" as a practical business case communications tool, and as a training tool. My experience showed me that the single biggest hurdle to overcome in turning TM into a profit center is attitude. It is critical not only that senior leaders change their perspective on TM, but also that every manager and employee involved in the TM function fully understands and buys into the concept. The sooner people see a clear connection between investments in TM and resultant benefits, the sooner they will begin to act differently. They will start to question old methods and procedures, and they will involve TM in more strategic discussions. They will measure TM contributions, hold TM accountable, and properly resource the function.

Strategic Talent Management

The PROFIT Model for Maximizing ROI in TM

P – Problem/ Profit Opportunity identification

The first step in any solution is to identify the problem (sales, staff turnover, productivity, union grievances, missed marketing opportunities, rate of absenteeism, wastage, down time of equipment, accidents and profitability).

R - Resources wasted (cost of problem)

While identifying the problem is very important, the context of the problem must also be described if the actual cost to the company is to be estimated. The greater the erosion of the bottom-line, the more urgently the problem needs to be addressed.

O – Opportunity for a Solution

This is where TM leaders have the opportunity and responsibility to prove their worth by creating specific solutions to address pressing problems. The failure of TM leaders to craft practical, creative solutions to such problems only reinforces the notion that TM is unimportant in the minds of CEOs and CFOs. Unless and until TM can prove its worth, senior leaders will always see TM as a cost center.

F - Financial investment required

This step is the determination of the financial investment that will be required to resolve the problem. This is a critical step, because it provides the all-important "where the rubber hits the road" check to make sure the solution is not more expensive than the problem.

I - Improvement generated

This step of the PROFIT model calculates the actual dollar amount of improvements directly generated by the TM solution.

T - Tracked ROI

This final step is the all-important measurement of the return on investment. It clearly indicates in a ratio format how much money was saved or generated as a direct result of implementing the solution. The higher the ratio, the better the ROI, and the more value TM brings to the bottom line.

The following is a blank template you can use. This book includes many case examples of clients I have helped over the years to illustrate how the PROFIT model works.

Note: When costing out a problem, solution or improvement be sure to take into account all relevant costs. It should also be noted that it is best to err on the conservative side when determining costs. That is, do not try to stretch or inflate the improvement generated. Instead, use real (third-party verifiable) figures that even the most cynical executives will support. Also, remember the straightforward philosophy of the PROFIT model: keep it simple, and resist the tendency to create more bureaucratic paperwork for others. *The true value of TM is not in how many trees get cut down to create paperwork, but in the measurable profits it creates for the company!*

Problem/ Profit Opportunity:
Resources wasted:
Opportunity for a Solution:
Financial investment required:
Improvement generated:
Tracked ROI:

Strategic Talent Management

TM Metrics

The following are some talent management questions for the topic of TM Metrics that you might want to consider adding to your TM Scoreboard.

- What TM Metrics are we currently using? Which ones should we be using?
- Have senior executives been trained on how to measure TM Investments and how they impact the bottom line?
- Are leaders held accountable (and rewarded) for TM Investments?
- Are TM investments and their impact on the bottom line discussed at Board of Directors meetings?
- Has your company adopted, or is it in the process of adopting, any of the 12 Agile Principles into your list of TM practices? If so, how smoothly has the process been implemented, and how have these measures impacted profits?
- Do leaders spend at least 30% of their time on talent issues? What percentage of a leader's compensation is tied to developing talent?
- What capabilities/competencies are most needed, both now and in the future? Have competencies been developed for every position, especially for leadership and strategic jobs?
- Is there adequate bench strength—two or more candidates currently ready—for all leadership and strategic positions throughout the organization?
- Does a direct link exist between a person's job and the business strategy and values of the organization?
- Is the contribution of each employee to the overall mission clear? What percentage of employees have their goals directly aligned with organizational goals?
- Is the best talent focused on the most strategic and critical roles in the organization?
- Other possible TM questions...

Chapter Two: Attracting and Selecting Exceptional Talent

> "
>
> **I've had good players and I've had bad players. I'm a better coach with good players.**
>
> Lou Holtz
>
> "

Recruiting is Broadcasting

Recruiting is an essential element of attracting quality employees. Recruiting is actually a form of marketing, since it's really a process of selling a job opportunity to prospective employees. Recruiters need to be honest about what the position entails, and avoid overselling candidates on the company; overselling can lead to disillusionment and, eventually, to staff turnover. It can also result in new recruits accusing the company of false advertising, a charge that can damage the firm's reputation and hamper future recruitment efforts.

Recruitment activity should be creative, imaginative, honest, and innovative. Proper word choice in recruiting materials is essential. For instance, avoid describing your company as simply old or big; descriptors like rapidly expanding, nationally known, or leading, are more dynamic, and are much more likely to appeal to quality candidates. In addition, the style of recruiting material should be simple and direct, always shedding light on the candidate's primary question of, "What's in it for me?" In this vein, do not forget to personalize your material by using pronouns like "you" and "your." Finally, you should never lose sight of the fundamental objectives of your recruitment campaign.

Strategic Talent Management

Typically, there are five main objectives for recruitment material:

1. To attract suitable candidates for the job
2. To eliminate inappropriate candidates
3. To motivate many appropriate candidates to apply
4. To reach the best people as economically as possible
5. To enhance the overall reputation of the company by the image projected in the recruitment material

No single recruitment technique is effective at all times, under all circumstances, and for all companies. Most companies have found they must be prepared to adapt their methods to the constantly changing nature of the labor market.

Timing is Everything

Dr. John Sullivan says that the timing of the recruiting message is as important as the message itself when targeting top prospects. He offers the following suggestions related to "right timing" under different circumstances.:

- Birthdays and New Year's Day are times of reflection

- A boss, mentor, best friend or CEO left the company

- Day of a merger or layoff announcement

- Lost a promotion or a key project

- After their yearly bonus

- After their performance appraisal

- When their project is ending

- Their annual work anniversary

Strategic Talent Management

TM Solution: Tapping into Near Free Labour

Case study: Small manufacturing company

Problem/ Profit Opportunity: Shortage of available funds to explore feasibility of new product line.

Resources wasted: About 8% down time in production time and equipment, assuming current production team of 18 people working 40 hours per week: 18 employees x 40 hours x $12/hour = $8,640 weekly labor costs @ 8% downtime = $691.20 per week or $35,942 per year.

Opportunity for a Solution: 1 college co-op placement student for a 3-month period, created feasibility study of new product line including surveying existing clients to gauge interest for new products.

Financial investment required: co-op student stipends and work-related expenses = $3,200.

Improvement generated: Reduced production downtime to 3% and generated $63,000 in gross margins with new sales.

Tracked ROI: 19.7:1.

Strategic Talent Management

TM Solution: "We Will Pump You Up!"

Case study: Small-sized manufacturing company.

Problem/ Profit Opportunity: High employee absenteeism and turnover (11 people turnover in prior year) for one position on all three production lines.

Resources wasted: Cost of turnover, overtime to cover absenteeism, and cost of supervisors covering vacant positions: $18,000.

Opportunity for a Solution: Survey of three current position holders and four previous ones that had left the company uncovered that the pallet stacking position was very physically demanding, entailing the lifting and placing of 50-lb boxes of packaged products quickly and neatly on pallets. The company was already paying a premium for this position, and the size and weight of the packages could not be changed because they were specs set by the client. The solution was to hire a weight-training instructor to analyze what type of a workout someone would get in a typical shift. Muscle groups used and calories burned were all determined. A campaign to promote the position as being similar to a paid visit to the gym was very well received by two of the three jobholders. A like-minded gym type replaced the third. To further encourage retention, the company gave $100 gift cards to a local vitamin shop for every three months each person stayed on the job. Two years later, the same three people were still there.

Financial investment required: Cost of weight trainer consulting: $1,000, plus cost of gift cards per year: $1,200. Total cost $2,200.

Improvement generated: Zero turnover and virtually no absenteeism.

Tracked ROI: 8.2:1.

Strategic Talent Management

TM Solution: Tapping into Free Electrons

Case study: Small manufacturing company.

Problem/ Profit Opportunity: High cost of ineffectively recruiting for operations manager position.

Resources wasted: Various recruiting methods had failed to attract quality candidates for the position. Total recruiting costs: $5,400 (ads in city newspaper, help wanted banner onsite).

Opportunity for a Solution: Created a Twitter account for the company and followed several dozen respected sector leaders (one of whom had over 12,000 followers). Tweeted the job opportunity, and several followers re-tweeted it. Hundreds of unique visitors subsequently visited the job section of the manufacturer's website, and 17 resumes were submitted. The position was filled within one week of the tweet.

Financial investment required: Zero cost to join Twitter, $100 paid to an employee's daughter (high school student) to coach president for several hours on how to set up and use Twitter.

Improvement generated: Hired a great operations manager for virtually no cost.

Tracked ROI: 54:1.

Strategic Talent Management

Table 2. Low-cost/high-impact recruiting ideas.

Source	Pros	Cons
Own staff (internal job postings)	• Individual is known • Helps keep employee • Develops current staff • Person has company knowledge • Low cost & time investment	• Limited choice • No "new blood" from outside of company • Staff may not have all required skills
Former staff (that you would like to rehire)	• Individual is known • Person has company knowledge	• Limited choice • Potential challenges with former employee or team mates
Social Media LinkedIn Facebook Twitter Instagram Pinterest	• Free or very inexpensive • Quick results • Build relationship via online engagement • Provides insight on applicants interests & personality • Expose discriminatory activity	• Missing or inaccurate information • Disqualifying a potential applicant with small online presence • Potential for massive number of candidates • Recruiters need to be social media savvy
Community newspaper ads/ Help wanted signs/ Banners / Bumper Sticker	• Quick method of reaching wide audience • Enhances company's brand image	• Shotgun approach lacks focus • Success depends on visibility • Limited space for information
Job/career fairs (sponsored by a community organization, YMCA, chamber of commerce)	• Time effective way of promoting job to many people • Excellent method of capturing passive job seekers' attention • Can conduct on-site interviews • Increase customers • Fair organizer handles marketing	• Can be expensive, time-consuming and require pre-planning • Difficult for small players to compete with "major players" • Requires marketing material • Too many fairs can lose job seekers' attention
Radio or television	• Quick method of reaching wide audience • If done well, can enhance brand image • If engaging, can attract attention of passive seeker	• Expensive • Requires lots of pre-planning • Shotgun approach lacks focus
Internet recruiting (your company webpage, on-line recruitment page, Monster.ca, Workopolis.ca, Hotjobs.ca, industry association, banner space)	• Very low cost of attracting high volume of applicants • Works 24/7 • Instant communication of message • Rapidly becoming one of the preferred methods of job search • Access to global market • Ease of updating/editing job postings • More space for additional information, photos & links to related sites. • Ease of applicant being able to apply online	• Massive volume of databases can be overwhelming • Requires candidates to be computer literate • Choosing best site out of thousands of online portals • Recruiters need to be comfortable with technology
Educational institutions (high school, trade schools, universities) career fairs, job boards, student employment center)	• Target people with specific qualifications • Tap into younger workers • Fulfill seasonal needs • Trial period for long-term employment • Co-op placements • Develop face-to-face relationship	• Often little previous relevant work experience • Difficult for small players to compete with "major players"
Walk-ins (plant, facility, retail)	• Available for work • Opportunity for "first impression" • Made the effort to appear in person	• Many may not be ideal candidates • Spur-of-moment/impulsive application

Strategic Talent Management

Employee Referrals

An employee referral occurs when an existing employee encourages one of their acquaintances to apply for a position in your company, or when your employee notifies you about a potential employee in their social network. By encouraging your workers to invite their friends and family to apply for work at your company, you are turning your entire team into recruiters who can sell your company—and its available positions—to some great candidates.

Benefits of creating an employee referral program

> **I have found that referred employees are 20–40% more productive when starting their new jobs than non-referred hires.**
>
> Dave Lefkow, Senior Director, Jobster

Your employees can be your best recruiters. Your company will enjoy many significant benefits by implementing a well-thought-out employee referral program. Research has shown that employees hired through referrals typically display the following positive qualities over their non-referred counterparts:

- Cost less to "reach," resulting in reduced advertising and search firm fees
- Take less time to recruit
- Have greater understanding of what the job entails
- Adapt more quickly to new job and to company culture
- Display higher levels of performance sooner
- Fit in more quickly with existing team
- Stay with companies for longer periods of time
- Attract like-minded people… agile thinkers attract other agile thinkers

Strategic Talent Management

> **Over 93% of the top performers in their field find a job by being referred by someone they know, not through a job posting.**
>
> Forbes

The main differences between working with a new hire who was referred by an employee, and one who was hired from the street OR hired off the street, are that the referred hire already has a realistic expectation of the job, has already been "endorsed" by your employee, and comes with a personal liaison to provide orientation to your company.

> **Referred employees stay at the job four times longer and are fired about four times less than employees who were not referred.**
>
> Prof. John Sullivan, San Francisco State University

How Referable is Your Company?

Imagine receiving very poor service and undercooked food at a restaurant. As you pay for your meal, the manager says, "I hope you will encourage your friends and family to come check us out. If they do, we will give you a coupon for a free appetizer." Note that the manager makes this offer without enquiring about the quality of the food and service you received. This example is similar to the way many companies implement employee referral programs. They offer a token referral bonus to encourage their employees to recruit friends and family members into an organization that is less than stellar. It should come as no surprise that this approach to employee referrals has unspectacular results.

Strategic Talent Management

It's all about the EXPERIENCE

If you want a more successful employee referral program, you first need to make sure you are giving your employees something to brag about.

The following slogan applies to both the world of customer service and to creating an organization that employees will be proud to share with others. "People will go to where they are *invited*, will stay when they are *appreciated*, and will *Invite* others when encouraged to do so!" To turn your workforce into a team of recruiters, you need to take an honest look at the work experience you deliver.

If you create the right EXPERIENCE, they will talk

By asking questions about the work experience you deliver to your employees, you will be able to design the kind of experience that employees want to tell others about. They will want to tell their friends and family because they feel so lucky, and they know how exceptional their employer is. They will want to give the people they care about and respect an opportunity to be as lucky as they are. Not only does creating such a satisfying, motivating, inspiring work experience turn your workforce into a band of head-hunters, it also improves morale, productivity, engagement, and customer service quality. So doing this is not a "nice to do if we had the time" project. Rather, it is a hard-headed measure with far-reaching implications for your financial viability.

The following tool is meant to provide you a quick analysis of how well your organization delivers in terms of ten key employee experiences.

Employee E.X.P.E.R.I.E.N.C.E.

Entering the organization (Onboarding)
X Exiting the organization
Performance Management & feedback
Engagement levels
Recruitment process
Individual development plan & mentoring
Employee Referrals
Networking with Colleagues
Communications with Supervisor
Equity in work/ life balance

Strategic Talent Management

Table 3 Self-check – 10 key employee E.X.P.E.R.I.E.N.C.E.s™

The following self-check will get you started with an analysis of the work experience your company delivers. Here is how to use it for maximum benefit:

1. Use the experiences as a starting point to generate a more complete checklist defining the total employee experience at your company.
2. Use the questions under each experience to analyze how you can improve the way you deliver that experience.

Entering the organization (Onboarding)	Yes	No
Is your orientation program inspiring?		
Does your onboarding program leave new hires with the impression that you're a well-run, professional outfit that does things right?		
Does your onboarding process lead to new hires feeling that they are valued, that their employer cares about their well being and success?		
Does your onboarding process reinforce the new employee's decision to work here vs. somewhere else?		
X Exiting the organization	**Yes**	**No**
Was the real reason for the person's leaving identified?		
Was every reasonable effort made for both parties to part on positive terms?		
Were opportunities for internal improvements noted, communicated and implemented?		
Performance Management & feedback	**Yes**	**No**
Do employees receive regular performance feedback?		
Do supervisors and managers know how to give feedback in clear, concrete terms?		
Do supervisors and managers know how to give corrective feedback respectfully?		
Do supervisors and managers know how to invite employees to share their point of view so they feel understood?		

Strategic Talent Management

	Yes	No
Do supervisors and managers integrate these conversations into the employee's individual development plan?		
Are performance evaluations seen as a useful performance enhancement and professional development tool?		
Does the performance evaluation reflect previous performance and detail the plan for moving forward?		
Are employees active participants in the review process, assessing their own performance?		
Engagement levels	**Yes**	**No**
Overall, are the employees very satisfied with their job?		
Overall, are the employees very satisfied with their employer?		
Overall, are the employees very satisfied with their boss?		
Overall, are the employees very satisfied with their co-workers?		
Recruitment process	**Yes**	**No**
Does your process attract the best and brightest candidates?		
Does your process leave applicants feeling respected?		
Does your process lead people to view your company as a well-run outfit?		
Does your process lead people to view your company as an employer who cares about and respects its employees?		
Does the job offer clearly state the job being offered (start date and time, pay and benefits)?		
Does the welcome package provide valuable information for the new recruit to review before the first day on the job?		
Individual development plan & mentoring	**Yes**	**No**
Does each employee have an individual development plan?		
Are individualized training need assessments conducted on each employee before training begins?		
Is a learning culture part of the organization?		
Does the company measure its ROI on training and development efforts?		

Strategic Talent Management

Employee Referrals	Yes	No
Is there a structured employee referral program in place?		
Are employees aware of the employee referral program?		
Is the process for referring someone easy to do?		
Does the company quickly act upon the referral provided, by contacting the referred person?		
Does the employee who provided the referral get acknowledged in some way?		
Is there a formalized process to provide thanks after a referral is given and a reward after new employee passes probation?		
Networking with Colleagues	**Yes**	**No**
Is cross-departmental communications among colleagues encouraged?		
Has every effort been made to ensure "silos" don't develop within the organization? If they develop are there removed?		
Are colleagues from distant locations networking via video conferencing not just email and text?		
Does a culture of mutual respect exist with all colleagues regardless of position?		
Can all employees access senior leaders?		
Does your colleague networking showcase people with high potential?		
Communications with Supervisor	**Yes**	**No**
Is it safe for employees to voice their disagreements with their boss?		
Is honesty and openness valued, supported, and encouraged?		
Do employee concerns get addressed?		
If an employee concern doesn't result in change, is an explanation provided?		
Are employee's ideas and input highly valued?		
Are employees advised of the status of their ideas? If an idea isn't used, do they understand why?		
Are managers coached about how to make it safe for employees to be open with them?		
Are managers held accountable for their behavior toward employees?		
Are employees kept in the loop during change processes?		

Equity in work/ life balance	Yes	No
Is work from home allowed (even part of the time)?		
Is the culture one in which employees are not expected to work after they leave work or is there a restriction on how many hours are expected of any employee in a given week?		
Is the focus on outcomes, not hours worked?		
Are healthy breaks (exercise, stretching or standing) promoted throughout the workday?		
Is extra time off for charitable pursuits or volunteer work offered?		
Do you ask employees what work/ life balance means to them and take reasonable steps to accommodate?		

3. Ask the following questions for each "E.X.P.E.R.I.E.N.C.E.":

   - *What do our employees say they want from each **E.X.P.E.R.I.E.N.C.E.** interaction?*
   - How do our employees feel and see things after dealing with each **E.X.P.E.R.I.E.N.C.E.** interaction as they are told?
   - How would our employees feel if we instructed them to deal with **E.X.P.E.R.I.E.N.C.E.** interactions differently?
   - What emotions and perceptions should we be trying to create in our employees, and what do we need to do to create them?

4. You can get the ball rolling by asking your employees, "Have you had the kind of work experience at our company that makes you want to tell others that we're a great place to work? "Do your experiences here make you want to recommend us to your friends and colleagues?

5. Make sure you involve employees not only in data gathering, but also in implementing changes. As for any change or corporate initiative, the more you involve your employees in the process, the more invested they'll be in it. Higher levels of investment result in better data, and better data leads to more productive recruitment of talent.

Strategic Talent Management

TM Solution: 100% of Staff are Recruiters

Case study: Small professional services firm.

Problem/ Profit Opportunity: Challenge of recruiting accountant to a firm in a small rural town.

Resources wasted: Costs for ad in national newspaper and placement with major e-recruitment portals (Monster, Workopolis): $15,000.

Opportunity for a Solution: Created an employee referral program, shared job description with each of 16 staff, and offered $2,000 referral bonus if referred candidate was hired and successfully completed a three-month probationary period.

Financial investment required: $2,000.

Improvement generated: Hired new accountant within 12 business days.

Tracked ROI: 7.5:1.

Give Me 5

Google uses a very direct approach to employee referrals called the "Give me 5." Under this policy, the company approaches top performers and asks them to identify the top five people that they know in their field in terms of performance, innovation, team orientation, management skill, and performance under pressure. the following categories:

- The best performer
- The most innovative
- The best team player
- The best manager
- The best at working under pressure

They then ask their top performers to reach out to these five individuals in an effort to try to convince them to apply for work at Google.

Strategic Talent Management

Pre-screening: Finding the Best People in the Crowds

> **Good people are found, not changed.**
>
> Jim Rohn

You've taken the time to attract a large pool of applicants, but you have only one position to fill. Are you going to interview all 92 salespeople? I hope not! You clearly must reduce the size of your applicant pool to three to five candidates. The best ways to screen applicants quickly include the following steps:

- Evaluate their resumes and cover letters
- Study their application forms
- Check their references
- Review their social media and online footprint

Pre-interview screening gives you an efficient way to assess each applicant's credentials and basic suitability. Follow-up interviews focus on character in an attempt to determine whether a particular candidate is the best person for a particular job.

A creative way to save time and energy in pre-screening is to tell applicants to personally drop off their resumes and cover letters at your office. This works well to weed out people for whom your company's location is a problem. For instance, some candidates may have difficulty simply finding your offices, or they may discover it is too long a commute, or that it requires too much in weekly parking fees. Only candidates who actually make it to your office without complaint should be provided a detailed job description. Some of these candidates, after reading the job description, may realize that they are not suited for the job when its location and detailed requirements are taken into account.

Strategic Talent Management

Imagine the time, energy, and money you can save if a large number of applicants screen themselves out in this manner. If the applicant wants to pursue the opportunity further, they should be asked to fill out a detailed application form, which should be considered to be a solid indicator of their level of interest. You may at this point also want to ask them to write a paragraph about themselves. This particular exercise isn't relevant to every position, but it will indicate competency in writing skills and penmanship.

Job Applications

The job application form is an efficient way to assess and compare each applicant's background, skills, knowledge, and key competencies in the context of the requirements of the job. The key questions for this tool are, *Can the applicant actually do the job? and Is the applicant competent for the job?*

There are a number of potential danger signs you should be looking for when reviewing applications. These warning signs include the following:

- An erratic job history, with several periods of unemployment or job-hopping.

- Major unexplained gaps in employment.

- Salary expectations that exceed the typical pay range for the position.

- Frequent changes of residence.

- Considerable detail regarding previous experience or education, which is irrelevant to the position.

- Reasons for leaving previous jobs that suggest there were some possible negative issues.

- Health challenges or physical disabilities that would prevent the individual from performing the duties of a specific job.

Cover Letters and Resumes

There's an old saying in advertising: "Let the buyer beware." The same holds true for recruiting. Remember that resumes provide a one-sided look at an applicant: the positive side. Resumes, by their very nature, help applicants put their best foot forward. Keep in mind that what is not said in the cover letter and resume is just as important as what is said.

Strategic Talent Management

Here are nine tips on what to look for when reviewing resumes:

1. **Does the applicant demonstrate a sense of achievement and accomplishment in their resume?** Past performance is a good indicator of future performance. If the person has a track record of being an achiever in the past, chances are that this trend will continue.

2. **Is the applicant profit- and cost-conscious?** Any candidate who suggests ways in which they might dramatically increase profits or reduce costs is someone worth a second look. One of the difficulties we often face is candidates who have the skills and knowledge to do a job, but who don't see their potential position in terms of the big picture. Such candidates may know how to do a job, but can't see beyond their narrow slice of responsibilities to the impact their work has on the overall financial well-being of the company.

3. **Is the candidate client-driven?** My friend, the late Bill Gibson, had a slogan he used often: "Everyone is in sales." It doesn't matter whether you're the president of the company, a janitor, or a receptionist: everyone, at one point or another, has to effectively market the good name of the company.

4. **Has the applicant demonstrated stability?** Stability and dependability are two issues that are near and dear to most leaders' hearts. I would urge caution before hiring anyone with a long history of changing jobs. There is little profit in being a stepping stone for someone else. On the other hand, anyone who has actually been able to change jobs frequently must possess some fairly strong abilities; how else could they have repeatedly sold themselves to various organizations? Look at the applicant, get a feel for what their goals are, compare them to what you're offering, and ask yourself: Will this job satisfy this person, or will they soon become disillusioned and disappointed, and continue their job-hopping?

5. **Is the applicant goal-oriented?** When I'm reviewing resumes, I take particular interest in the personal and professional goals the applicant has described. What I'm looking for is someone who has a burning desire to win.

6. **Does the applicant have a solid work ethic?** Although it's difficult to determine the strength of a candidate's work ethic from their resume alone, you can certainly get clues. For instance, I consider any candidate who mentions numerous volunteer positions for worthwhile endeavors as someone who is probably prepared to go that extra mile. Another strong indicator of a solid work ethic is an indication that a candidate's performance in a previous position exceeded the actual requirements of the job. On the other hand, you should be cautious whenever you sense a candidate's reluctance to take on anything not explicitly covered in the job description, especially if that reluctance is coupled with an inflexible attitude.

7. **How much information has the applicant disclosed in their resume?** Has the applicant "beefed up" the personal section with a long list of interests and hobbies? If so, this may indicate someone who'd rather play than work, or someone who doesn't have a lot of experience. Other red flags are the frequent use of phrases like, "has experience at," "has knowledge of," "has assisted with," or "is familiar with." These vague phrases often represent an attempt to inflate a skimpy skill-set. When I see phrases like this and question the candidate directly about their experience, I usually find that they lack hands-on experience.

8. **What is the applicant's attitude?** A resume containing comments like, "I didn't really enjoy this," or, "It was so-and-so's fault," almost always reflects a candidate with a negative attitude. I would suggest you trash these applications immediately. Candidates who are overtly negative and bitter in their resumes are unlikely to be the sort of person we want on our team.

9. **Look for substance, not style.** Although a book with an attractive cover will warrant a second look, it doesn't guarantee a sale. This is also true for resumes. Be on guard for "slick" resumes. Look beyond the surface appearance to the actual information it contains.

Once you've gone through all the resumes, the next step is to screen them. One of the quickest methods is to divide the pile into three smaller ones representing "yes," "maybe," and "no." Set up interviews with the "yes" applicants, send rejection letters to the "no" applicants, and place the "maybes" in a pending file to be used as a backup.

Reference Checking

Unfortunately, many people lie on their resumes. Some claim to have university degrees they never received, while others claim to have worked for companies that never employed them. The best way to guard against such falsifications is to check the references.

It is a little-known fact that 90% of all hiring mistakes can be prevented through proper reference-checking. Unfortunately, the vast majority of recruiters do not take the time to do this, relying instead on their own impression or "gut" feeling after reviewing the cover letter, resume, application form, and interview. This is a mistake. As I've mentioned before, hiring the wrong person can be very costly.

Checking references is absolutely essential. It's estimated that one third of all job applicants either lie or exaggerate on their resumes, cover letters, or application forms.

Interviews: Getting to Know Each Other

The main reason for a selection interview is to figure out which of your pre-screened candidates is the best person for the job. But there is also another purpose: for you to familiarize the applicant with the opportunities in your company. A thought to keep foremost in your mind is that the interview is intended to narrow down the number of likely prospects for a specific position. As an interviewer, you should ask yourself two key questions:

- "How well will the applicant fit in with my company?"
- "To what degree will my company benefit if this candidate is hired?"

Although interviews are usually conducted on a one-to-one basis between the interviewer and the candidate, group interviews are also sometimes used. One form of group interview is to have the applicant meet with two or more interviewers. These interviewers could be the department heads or peers that the recruit would be working with on the job. This format allows each interviewer to evaluate each candidate on the basis

Strategic Talent Management

of the same questions and answers, thereby increasing the reliability of impressions formed during the interview.

Online interviews provide low-cost alternatives to initial face-to-face interviews, especially when factoring in the high cost of travel. Through web-based apps such as Skype, both parties can be brought together in virtual face-to-face contact.

Another variation is to have two or more applicants interviewed together by one or more interviewers. This saves time, especially for busy executives. It also allows the answers from different applicants to be compared immediately.

Competency-based Interviews

Competency-based interviews (often referred to as behavioral interviews) are the most reliable way to identify applicants who have the competencies critical to exemplary job performance and your company's success.

Competency interviews focus on past behaviors, asking candidates how they handled certain situations previously. The underlying premise is that past behavior is predictive of future behavior.

How Competency-based Interviews Work

It's important to have a basic conceptual understanding of behavioral/competency interviewing in order to do it. An interviewer conducting a competency-based interview must first identify the critical competencies associated with performing a specific job, and then assess each candidate in terms of these abilities.

Traditional hiring systems are often based on the technical qualifications for a job, and traditional interviews often focus on detailed discussions of job experience. These interviews are often based on several "stock" questions, such as:

- What are your strengths and weaknesses?
- What could you bring to our organization?
- Why do you want this job?
- What do you think makes you the best candidate for this job?

Selection decisions are often based on the "emotional attraction" of the applicant to the interviewer—which is to say, on which candidate the interviewer likes best, or which candidate seems to have a work style that most complements the style of the interviewer. Formal education, technical knowledge, and experience are important job qualifications, but they are often considered as nothing more than threshold requirements. By contrast, a candidate's attitudes, motivations, and behavioral characteristics (*competencies*) are considered to be much more predictive of superior performance.

During a behavioral interview, interviewers ask the applicant competency-based questions intended to elicit information about how the applicant demonstrated competency in the past. For example, in a behavioral interview focusing on the competency of *customer focus*, the interviewer might ask the following series of questions:

- Can you tell me about a specific situation where a client (customer) became angry with you because you were unable to provide what he or she wanted?

- How did you handle it?

- How did the situation turn out?

The interviewer could then continue to probe for details providing insight into how the candidate can be expected to handle difficult customer service interactions in the future.

Developing a Competency-based Interviewing Process

The steps to develop a competency interviewing process include identifying specific competencies to assess, developing and asking appropriate interview questions, and scoring or grading competency-based interviews.

Step 1: Identify Targeted Competencies

There are two basic guidelines to follow in identifying specific competencies to target during behavioral interviews:

1. Identify a reasonable number of competencies to focus on, and the number of questions to probe each competency.

2. Choose the type of job competencies that are most difficult to develop in an employee.

Strategic Talent Management

Experienced interviewers find it is best to ask two or three questions for each job competency, as well as probing follow-up questions. Experienced interviewers find it better to conduct an in-depth interview on six to eight truly key competencies than to attempt a broad-brush interview covering all factors that might possibly affect job performance.

Step 2: Develop and Ask the Right Interview Questions

The next step is to develop questions designed to provide as much information as possible about the applicant's experience in each competency. In essence, you will be inviting applicants to "tell their story" about a specific situation in the past in which they exhibited a particular competency.

Each question should elicit three specific pieces of information:

- A description of the situation.
- The applicant's role, responsibility, or action in the situation or incident.
- The specific outcome of the situation or incident.

For the Stress Tolerance competency, an example of a three-part question might be as follows:

1. **Situation** – Sometimes tensions run high in the kind of work we do. Can you describe a stressful situation or interaction you have had with a supervisor in the past?
2. **Role/responsibility/action** – What did you do? How did you respond?
3. **Outcome** – What happened? What was the final outcome?

Step 3: Score and Evaluate Competency-based Interviews

Finally, you need to evaluate the applicant's answers and rate the applicant for the competencies you selected in Step 1.

Techniques for conducting competency interviews

- **Try to put the applicant at ease.** The initial step in any good job interview is to help the applicant feel comfortable in what is usually a stressful situation. A few minutes of "small talk" usually breaks the ice. Since many applicants have never participated in a behavioral interview, it is helpful to briefly explain the process at the beginning of the interview.

- **Reassure applicants if they have trouble recalling specific examples.** Some applicants will have a hard time thinking of specific examples. Encourage them to take some time to think about the question. Remind applicants with little work experience that examples from their college experience or their personal life are appropriate. If an applicant appears to be stuck on a particular question, offer to ask the next question and come back to this question later in the interview. Often, examples that come up in later questions trigger an example that illustrates the candidate's response to a scenario probed earlier.

- **Keep the applicant focused on the specifics.** Some applicants have a tendency to speak in generalities. Watch for phrases like, "I always," I usually," and "I never." Respond by asking for specifics, by redirecting the applicant with phrases like, "We're looking for a specific situation," or "Can you give a specific example of that?"

- **Keep the applicant focused on what he or she did.** Some applicants tend to use the word "we" even when talking about something done individually. Since it is very important to clearly understand precisely what the applicant did, you may need to keep reminding the applicant that you are only interested in what he or she did. Offering an explanation of why the applicant needs to use the word "I" usually helps.

- **Focus the Applicant on Facts Rather than Opinions.** Some applicants couch their answers in the context of what they believe, rather than what they did. If the applicant makes statements such as "Clients are always my top priority," you should respond by asking them to provide a concrete example.

- **Keep the Applicant Focused on Past Behaviours.** Even if you ask for a specific example, some applicants may respond as if they were asked a hypothetical question. Simply remind the applicant that you need specific examples from the past.

Using a competency library to create a job description

I define competencies as the knowledge, skills, behaviors, personal attributes, and other characteristics that are associated with or predictive of superior job performance. The following Competency Library can be a useful starting place to narrow your list of competencies for a specific job to the eight to twelve that differentiate the best performers from the rest.

Strategic Talent Management

Competency Library - Adapted From CPSHR Services

- **Action-oriented:** Consistently maintains high levels of activity or productivity. Sustains long working hours when needed. Works with vigor, effectiveness, and determination over a sustained period.
- **Adaptability** (do not use with Facilitating Change): Adapts well to changes in assignments and priorities. Adapts behavior or work methods in response to new information, changing conditions, or unexpected obstacles. Approaches change positively and adjust behaviors accordingly.
- **Applied learning** (do not use with Continuous Learning and Professional Development): Able to learn and properly apply new job-related information in a timely manner. Has the ability to absorb and comprehend job-related information from formal training and other formal and informal learning experiences.
- **Building trust:** Interacts with others in a way that gives them confidence in one's motives and representations and those of the organization. Is seen as direct and truthful. Keeps confidences, promises, and commitments.
- **Coaching:** Provides timely guidance and feedback to help others strengthen knowledge/skills in areas needed to accomplish a task or solve a problem.
- **Collaboration:** Builds constructive working relationships with clients/customers, other work units, community organizations, and others to meet mutual goals and objectives. Behaves professionally and supportively when working with individuals from a variety of ethnic, social, and educational backgrounds.
- **Communication:** Clearly conveys and receives information and ideas through a variety of media to individuals or groups in a manner that engages the listener, helps them understand and retain the message, and invites response and feedback. Keeps others informed as appropriate. Demonstrates good written, oral, and listening skills
- **Conflict management:** Uses appropriate interpersonal styles and techniques to reduce tension and/or conflict between two or more people. Able to size up situations quickly. Able to identify common interests. Facilitates resolution.

Strategic Talent Management

- **Continuous learning and professional development** (do not use with Applied Learning): Is committed to developing professionally, attends professional conferences, focuses on best practices, and values cutting-edge practices and approaches. Takes advantage of a variety of learning activities, introduces newly gained knowledge and skills on the job.

- **Cultural competence:** Cultivates opportunities through diverse people. Respects and relates well to people from varied backgrounds, understands diverse world-views, and is sensitive to group differences. Sees diversity as an opportunity, challenges bias and intolerance.

- **Customer/client focus:** Makes customers/clients and their needs a primary focus of one's actions. Shows interest in and understanding of the needs and expectations of internal and external customers (including direct reports). Gains customer trust and respect. Meets or exceeds customer expectations.

- **Decision making/problem solving:** Breaks down problems into components and recognizes interrelationships. Makes sound, well-informed, and objective decisions. Compares data, information, and input from a variety of sources to draw conclusions. Takes action that is consistent with available facts, constraints, and probable consequences.

- **Delegating responsibility:** Comfortably delegates responsibilities, tasks, and decisions. Appropriately trusts others to perform. Provides support without removing responsibility.

- **Developing others:** Focuses on guiding others in accomplishing work objectives. Rewards and recognizes others, both formally and informally, in ways that motivate them. Sets high performance expectations for team members. Sets clear performance expectations and objectives. Holds others accountable for achieving results. Successfully finds resources, training, tools, etc. to support staff needs. Works with staff to create developmental opportunities to expand knowledge and skill level. Provides effective feedback and guidance for career development.

- **Facilitating change** (do not use with Adaptability): Facilitates the implementation and acceptance of change within the workplace. Encourages others to seek opportunities for different and innovative approaches to addressing problems and opportunities.

Strategic Talent Management

- **Follow-up:** Monitors the work of direct reports to ensure quality standards and thoroughness. Considers the knowledge, experience, and skill of staff members when determining extent of review.
- **Formal presentation skills:** Effectively presents ideas, information, and materials to individuals and groups. Effectively prepares and provides structured delivery. Facilitates workshops or meetings in a structured manner. Can facilitate and manage group processes.
- **Influence:** Uses appropriate interpersonal skills and techniques to gain acceptance for ideas or solutions. Uses influencing strategies to gain genuine agreements. Seeks to persuade rather than force solutions or impose decisions or regulations.
- **Initiative:** Takes action without being asked or required to. Achieves goals beyond job requirements. Is proactive. Takes prompt action to accomplish objectives.
- **Innovation:** Uses creativity and imagination to develop new insights into situations, and applies new solutions to problems. Comes up with new and unique ideas.
- **Managing work** (For supervisory competency. For non-supervisors, use Planning and Organizing): Shows ability to plan, schedule, direct work of self and others. Balances task requirements and individual abilities. Organizes materials to accomplish tasks. Sets challenging yet achievable goals for self and others.
- **Negotiation:** Effectively explores alternatives and positions to reach agreements and solutions that gain the support and acceptance of all parties.
- **Planning and organizing** (For non-supervisory competency. For supervisors, use Managing Work): Organizes work, sets priorities, and determines resource requirements. Determines necessary sequence of activities needed to achieve goals.
- **Quality orientation:** Monitors and checks work to meet quality standards; demonstrates a high level of care and thoroughness; checks work to ensure completeness and accuracy.
- **Risk taking:** Seeks opportunities and calculates risks to accomplish results that can lead to substantial benefit, knowing the real possibility of significant negative consequences.

Strategic Talent Management

- **Safety awareness:** Is aware of conditions and circumstances that affect one's own safety or the safety of direct reports.
- **Strategic focus:** Understands how an organization must change in light of internal and external trends and influences. Keeps the big, long-range picture in mind. Builds a shared long-range organizational vision with others. Commits to course of action to achieve long-range goals and influences others to translate vision into action.
- **Stress tolerance:** Maintains effective performance under pressure. Handles stress in a way that is acceptable to others and to the organization.
- **Team leadership** (For supervisory competency. For non-supervisors, use Teamwork): Communicates a vision and inspires motivation. Engages others (direct reports and peers) in team process to solve problems. Works to find a win/win resolution of differences. Is aware of how management style impacts staff productivity and development. Modifies leadership style to meet situational requirements. Helps team stay focused on major goals while managing within a context of multiple directives.
- **Teamwork** (For non-supervisory competency. For supervisors, use Team Leadership): Participates as an active and contributing member of a team to achieve team goals. Works cooperatively with other team members, involves others, shares information as appropriate, and shares credit for team accomplishments.
- **Technical/professional knowledge and skills:** Possesses, acquires, and maintains the technical/professional expertise required to do the job effectively and to create client/customer solutions. Technical/professional expertise is demonstrated through problem solving, applying professional judgment, and competent performance.
- **Visionary leadership:** Keeps the organization's mission, vision, and values at the forefront of employee decision-making and actions. Ensures alignment of organization's strategic plan and agency practices with vision, mission, and values.
- **Work standards:** Sets high standards and well-defined, realistic goals for one's self. Displays a high level of effort and commitment towards completing assignments in a timely manner. Works with minimal supervision. Is motivated to achieve.

Strategic Talent Management

Sample competency-based interview questions

Competency: Adaptability	
Please describe a significant change you have had to deal with at work recently.	
Possible follow-up questions:	What was your initial reaction to the change? What was your overall response? How did it all work out?
Notes:	

Competency: Building Trust	
Please tell us about a situation where you found it challenging to build a trusting relationship with another individual?	
Possible follow-up questions:	How did you go about doing it? How did it work out?
Notes:	

Competency: Collaboration	
Please describe a time when you formed an ongoing working relationship or partnership with someone from another department to achieve a mutual goal.	
Possible follow-up questions:	What did you do to make the relationship work? How has it worked out?
Notes:	

Competency: Continuous Learning and Professional Development	
Please describe what you have done to grow professionally in the recent past.	
Possible follow-up questions:	Did you apply what you learned on the job? How? What was the outcome?
Notes:	

Competency: Cultural Competence	
Please describe a time when you needed to be particularly sensitive to another person's beliefs, cultural background, or way of doing things?	
Possible follow-up questions:	What were the circumstances? What did you do? How did the situation work out?
Notes:	

Strategic Talent Management

Competency: Decision Making/Problem Solving	
Please describe a really difficult decision you had to make at work recently?	
Possible follow-up questions:	How did you go about making the decision? What alternatives did you consider? How did it turn out?
Notes:	

Competency-based interview questions

Competency:	
Possible follow-up questions:	
Notes:	

Competency:	
Possible follow-up questions:	
Notes:	

Competency-based Interview Evaluation. This table evaluates an Applicant for a position on the basis of responses provided to an interviewer (as summarized in the first two rows of the table). Review the characteristics listed in the "Element" column, and then rate the applicant based on interview responses. Place an "X" in box that best fits your assessment. Finally, at the bottom of the page, make one overall rating of the candidate based on a continuous scale in which 1 is unfavorable and 5 is favorable.

Applicant	Position	Interviewer

Table 4. Competency-based interview evaluation.

Element	1	2	3	4	5
The relevance of the candidate's work experience. Comments:					
The relevance of the candidate's education and training. Comments:					
The candidate's character, personality and overall attitude in relation to the job. Comments:					
Competency:					
Competency:					
Competency:					
Competency:					
Competency:					
Competency:					
Competency:					
Competency:					
Overall rating of candidate					

Note: You might consider having a second person (manager, TM specialist, or the supervisor of the position you are hiring for) join you during the interview. It's a great idea to have input from two people on how well the candidate will fit in with the company. Each interviewer should have their own copy of this tool and fill it in by themselves before discussing their rating of the applicant. This will prevent one interviewer from influencing the other's rating.

After you have successfully completed the interviewing stage of the recruiting process, you should have identified the best person for the position. The final step is to make the job offer and have both parties agree on the compensation package.

The next part of this book focuses on the issue of engaging and retaining exceptional people.

Strategic Talent Management

TM Metrics

The following TM Questions are relevant to attracting and selecting exceptional people who you might want to add to your TM Scoreboard.

- Are we seen as "an employer of choice"?
- Are we on "best places to work" lists?
- Is our recruiting campaign attracting "first-choice" candidates?
- What percentage of candidates do hiring managers consider to be superior to existing employees?
- What percentage of candidates do hiring managers consider unqualified?
- What percentage of first-choice candidates accepts our offers?
- Which recruiting sources provide candidates with the highest potential?
- What is our average time and cost to hire?
- How many key and hard-to-fill jobs remain vacant?
- What percentage of employees participates in referral programs, and what percentage of total hires are the result of employee referrals?
- Other possible TM questions…

Chapter Three: Engaging and Retaining Exceptional Talent

> " The largest single source of failed promotion is the failure to think through and help others prepare for a new job.
>
> Peter Drucker "

⚠ Danger

A recent Global workforce study of 90,000 respondents by Towers Perrin discovered that 21% of the employees surveyed were engaged with their work, 32% were neutral, and 47% were disengaged. These findings should be assessed in terms of the massive opportunity cost of the "engagement gap" between the discretionary effort needed by companies to remain agile, and effort that most employees are actually willing to put forth.

Strategic Talent Management

DID YOU KNOW

The three levels of employee engagement are defined as follows:

- **Engaged**—Seek and solve problems, and encourage others to do the same.
- **Satisfied**—Merely try to meet expectations; a passive state of contentment within an employee's comfort zone.
- **Disengaged:** Actively disinterested; a toxic mindset that creates problems within the organization.

The constant disruption associated with the unprecedented rate of change in the way we do business has forced organizations to seek any strategic advantage they can find. A struggling business can transform itself into a global leader by leveraging technology, or tapping into new markets, or creating new methods of distribution. Owners and senior managers of companies on the competitive edge are intensely concerned with the issue of engaging and retaining top employees. Their concern is warranted in light of the fact that implementing any major initiative requires total buy-in and support of highly engaged, competent people.

Throughout my entire career as a trainer, speaker and consultant, I have researched the best practices to engage, develop, and retain the best people. I have distilled all of the insights and lessons I have learned into what I call the "**F.A.C.T.S. of Engaging and Retaining Exceptional People.**" The following is a visual overview of the five most important factors job candidates seek in an ideal employer.

Flexibility and autonomy of work arrangements
Appreciation, recognition, rewards and frequent feedback
Challenging and interesting work that develops mastery
Trusting relationships
Salary, benefits and bonuses

I refer to these factors by the acronym F.A.C.T.S. because, in my years of working closely with tens of thousands of employees, I have consistently seen that these same five issues drive employee engagement. There are hundreds if not thousands of models and theories that purport to explain how employees can be engaged by their work. Some of these models are quite convoluted and confusing, while others are too simplistic. That being said, there are dozens of solid models that have stood the test of time. My model incorporates some of the best features of these classics, while also incorporating the personal insights I have gleaned from my decades of experience as a hands-on talent manager and consultant. If your organization consistently delivers the F.A.C.T.S. to every employee, you will be rewarded by a highly engaged team that will boost your profits regardless of the degree of economic disruption in the market.

Flexibility and Autonomy of Work Arrangements

The need for flexible working conditions is growing. The changing context of work is creating new challenges and opportunities that can only be dealt with by implementing flexible working arrangements.

The most common forms of flexible working are:

- Part-time working
- Home working
- Job sharing
- Variable hours
- Compressed hours
- Sabbaticals / Career breaks
- Staggered start / end times
- Dual roles
- Flexible Benefits (buying / selling holiday time)

Strategic Talent Management

Flexible working arrangements allow companies to meet present and future disruptive challenges by creating choice, accommodating generations, enabling complexity, and creating agility. Companies can reduce their carbon footprint and spare their staff from the fatigue of long distance travel by implementing various flexible work arrangements. Flexible work arrangements also reduce the need for expensive office space and corporate parking costs, while saving employees the cost and time of commuting. This flexibility allows for greater work/life balance because employees can attend to such important personal issues as child or elder care and volunteering while still ensuring that their work is being completed. Virtual teams comprised of staff from remote locations can deliver increased client expectations by providing 24/7 global customer care. Flexible and autonomous work arrangements with mature, responsible people can increase employee engagement, loyalty and retention.

> **If you are comfortable with the amount of freedom you have given your employees then you haven't gone far enough.**
>
> Larry Page, CEO Google

Agile Talent Management in its truest form is about giving everyone **autonomy** (the power) and **flexibility** (the freedom to choose how, when and where they work). Numerous studies have shown that workplace flexibility and autonomy are the two most important predictors of workplace satisfaction. Whether it is control of one's place and time of work, or of the work environment, autonomy and flexibility help engage and retain the best and brightest staff. New employees at Facebook are allowed to choose the team they want to join upon completion of their onboarding program. Facebook has also done away with tracking employee absenteeism. At Zappos, a concept called "**holacracy**" has replaced hierarchical structure with a series of self-governed teams that share authority and increase the speed and innovation of decision making. Netflix's approach to managing vacation time is, "there is no policy on tracking vacation time."

Appreciation, Recognition, Rewards and Frequent Feedback

One of the most powerful ways to engage and retain great people is to tap into appreciation, recognition, rewards and other forms of frequent feedback.

Everyone wants feedback; in fact, human beings crave it. Consider the various recreational activities we pursue outside of work; whether it's sports, online video games, or an old school board game, we all keep score. The score is direct feedback of how well we played. We all want feedback, *especially* positive feedback. One of the challenges of a workplace is that sometimes the only time we get feedback from our supervisors is when something has gone wrong. One of the cautions I give my clients is not to get involved in what I call "Peek-a-boo management." This is a management style in which supervisors keep a low profile, spying on their employees until somebody messes up, and they can spring a *Gotcha!* on them.

True, if an employee is doing something wrong, the improper behavior must be corrected immediately, before it has a chance to become a habit. However, looking at the feedback imperative from a positive perspective, one might more profitably concentrate on catching employees when they do something right. This is the opinion Ken Blanchard put forth in his classic book, *The One-Minute Manager*. It is my opinion as well. It is in fact imperative that Management should concentrate deliberately on catching their staff when *they do the right thing*. This kind of positive feedback does not merely mean saying, *Good job!* It should be much more expansive and explicit. It might consist of a manager telling an employee something that begins as follows: "Let me tell you specifically what you did right, what I liked about it, and the positive effect it had on the organization." If you take the time to do this, your employees will love the feedback process. The recognition you provide will strengthen the rapport between you and your team and, even more importantly, it will powerfully reinforce the positive behavior.

Strategic Talent Management

Performance feedback can run the formality spectrum from an impromptu micro-chat to the annual/semi annual performance appraisal meeting. Feedback sessions of all degrees of formality can provide useful positive reinforcement or redirection of improper behavior. All meaningful employee feedback must either reinforce positive behavior, turning it into a good habit, or redirect as employee's behavior into more desirable forms while strengthening the relationship between the leader and the employee. Regardless of the formality of the feedback session, there are two important and often overlooked principles that can greatly impact the session: the Sandwich technique and the Rule of 30/70.

The Sandwich technique of providing feedback has been around for years. Although it is not appropriate for every feedback discussion, it does provide a simple yet powerful way to give an employee a "creatively mixed message." Specifically, the sandwich technique allows the manager to acknowledge and commend several key behaviors or competencies while, at the same time, calling the employee's attention to one or more areas that should be improved. It is called the sandwich approach because the areas of strength are seen as the two outer buns, while the meat in the middle represents the area or opportunity for growth or improvement. The sandwich also serves as a visual reminder of the order in which the feedback should be provided. You put your employee at ease and gain a measure of trust by starting off with a sincere acknowledgement of several things an employee does well. Sharing positive feedback first will help them see the reality of the opportunities for their growth and development as an employee—the meat in the middle of the feedback sandwich. Once you have explored the area needing development and received a commitment from the employee, then close off the meeting with a "second bun," by sharing another positive behavior that you have observed. This will end the feedback session on an upbeat note. If, however, you have already used the sandwich technique in an unsuccessful attempt to redirect a teammate's performance, you may wish to skip the positive portion (reinforcement) of the feedback and focus on the redirection (meat).

Strategic Talent Management

One of the cautions when doing a feedback session is to avoid monopolizing the airtime by doing all of the talking. There is an old adage that states, "If you are talking, you are not listening, and if you are not listening, you are not learning." Yes, as the leader, coach or mentor, you do have valuable things to offer the employee; you do want to provide feedback, but you can't do that effectively by doing all of the talking. If you begin to dominate the conversation, the normal reaction is for the other person to disengage. In a feedback discussion we want the employee to open up, to get engaged, and to take responsibility for his or her behavior and professional growth.

The 30/70 rule contends that the ideal proportion of employee talking in a performance interview context is 70%, and therefore that the ideal verbal contribution of the interviewer is 30%. The more you can get your employees talking about their problem areas, and the more you can elicit specific improvement strategies from them, the more likely they will become committed to improving their performance. Quiet employees may give you the impression that getting them to talk for most of a meeting would be akin to pulling teeth. But that doesn't have to be the case if you use the "Ask vs. Tell" approach. The Ask vs. Tell approach makes use of open-ended questions, or questions that cannot be answered by a simple yes or no. When an interviewer poses open-ended questions, the responses will shed light on the interviewee's approach to thinking, problem solving, and the overall attitude towards the issue being discussed.

Example:

Paul, I just wanted to chat with you for a few moments about how things are going in the Williams retail showroom project. I noticed that over the past month you have been able to reduce the weekly project team meeting from about 2.5 hours to around one hour, and you are still managing to cover all of the agenda items. I think that is a smart and effective use of everyone's time. It would be fantastic if, moving forward, we can continue to have such productive project meetings. I was wondering how you have been able to do this? How you were able to keep everyone on track given the tendency of several team members to stray from the agenda?

In this first part of the meeting—the first bun of the sandwich—the leader is providing praise and reinforcement feedback. The next part is the asking of open-ended questions which, depending on the initial response, could lead to additional open-ended questions to probe the issue more deeply.

The meaty middle part of the sandwich might go something like this:

I also want to bring up a concern I have about the change in behavior I have noticed in Fred, one of your teammates. What behavioral changes have you noticed with him lately? How do you think his withdrawal from participating in the last two brainstorming sessions will affect the team? How do you think his withdrawn behavior will impact the project? As his project leader, you are responsible for establishing the environment for the team and for providing feedback to your people. What do you think is causing this change in him? What is he prepared to do to resolve this? What are you prepared to do to support him to resolve it? How long are you giving him to resolve it? What are you going to do if he doesn't resolve it?

This part of the feedback session focuses on re-directing Fred's behavior. By asking a number of open-ended questions, the leader hopes to uncover the real cause of Fred's behavior, whether it is coming from Fred and/or the Project Manager. The questions also seek a clear timeline to remedy the situation, and to force the Project Manager to make an explicit commitment to getting Fred back on track.

The final part, the second bun, would be to wrap up the feedback session with another reinforcement point.

Paul, as I mentioned I am very happy with the efficiency of the meetings, and I also want to congratulate you on your innovative suggestion of changing the layout of the room. By going open concept, you have saved our client tens of thousands of dollars in construction, and created a more dramatic atmosphere to showcase the power wall. The client is delighted with the proposed changes. Let's reconnect in a few weeks to see how things are going with Fred. Keep up the great work!

Strategic Talent Management

The following chart illustrates the keys steps in providing feedback.

Table 5. Steps in Providing Feedback.

Preparation	Consider:
	• How is this person performing?
	• In what ways does their work, behavior or actions meet/not meet your expectations?
	• Is the purpose of this meeting to reinforce or redirect behavior?
	• Have you been clear with the employee in the past about your expectations regarding this behavior?
	• Do they understand what is expected of them?
	• Is there a performance plan already in place, and is it relevant to the immediate discussion?
	• Schedule sufficient time for the one-on-one meeting, and book a quiet room without interruptions.
	• Rehearse (in your mind) the conversation beforehand.
Introduction	• Begin the conversation by explaining the purpose of the meeting.
	• Lay out the structure of the meeting.
	• Agree on standards of behavior required during the meeting.
	• Adopt a calm and professional manner.
	• Reassure them about confidentiality – prior to and after the meeting.
	• Don't be afraid to refer to your notes; they will keep you on track.
	• Remember to focus on the issue and not the person.
	• Maintain eye contact and a positive attitude.
Provide Reinforcement Feedback	1. Describe the behavior or performance you want to reinforce. Give specific examples and refer to dates, documents, work or specific interactions.
	2. Explain the positive impact that the behavior had on the organization.
	3. Help your employee to take credit for his or her success.
	4. Encourage your employee to continue the behavior.

Provide Redirection Feedback	1. Describe the behavior or performance (don't focus on personality traits) you want to re-direct. Focus on consistent behaviors and frequent incidents, rather than one-off examples of good or bad behavior. Use clear and simple words; do not use jargon or vague language.
	2. Listen to the reaction from your employee. Give the employee a few minutes to reflect on the feedback once you have delivered the review, and ask for questions or thoughts.
	3. The employee may agree that there is a problem and take responsibility for it. If they do this move on to step four. If new evidence emerges, adjourn the meeting if this feels appropriate. Or you may need to clarify your expectations for your employee's behavior or performance. If the employee rejects responsibility, explain the negative effect their actions are having on the organization or fellow coworkers.
	4. Help your employee take responsibility for issue(s).
	5. Guide your employee to develop a plan to adjust their behaviors. Be prepared to offer suggestions for improvements.
	6. Obtain a commitment and set a follow-up date to ensure the new behavior is taking hold. Document any agreement and give a copy to the employee.
	This should set out:
	• Agreed outcomes with dates and standards required.
	• Any support or training to be provided by the manager.
	• Any consequences if the agreement is breached.
	Remember: If this issue has occurred in the past you should have already spoken to the employee informally about the behavior – there should be no surprises during the one-on-one meeting.

Formal Performance Assessment and Development Discussion Checklist

The following checklist is designed to guide the supervisor in preparing, conducting, and following through on employee performance assessment and development discussions.

Strategic Talent Management

Before the meeting:

- Choose a time and place to hold the meeting that will minimize work disruption for supervisor and employee.
- Tell the employee well in advance of the meeting and explain process.
- Give employee enough time to prepare.
- Allow enough time for a two-way open discussion.
- Gather all necessary examples and documents relating to performance.

During the meeting:

- Provide employee with questions to be discussed at the meeting.
- Always start and end on a positive note.
- Focus on employee's performance and behaviors, not their personality.
- Use real examples of behaviors you have observed.
- Don't allow outside interruptions during the meeting.
- Always encourage employee to provide their point of view on the issue being discussed.
- Don't gloss over or make excuses for problems.
- Encourage employee to suggest ways to improve.
- Be positive and supportive when providing constructive criticism.
- Set a time to follow up discussion in the future.

The key thing when providing performance feedback is to do so in a timely, constructive, positive manner. The following self-check tool provides excellent feedback on the supervisor's ability to assess the performance of their employees.

Self-check: Assessing on-the-job performance

Read each statement and score it on a scale ranging from 1 (totally inaccurate) to 10 (totally accurate). The higher the number, the more the statement reflects you. Then add up the total of all of your scores.

Table 6. A self-assessment of on-the-job performance.

Statements	Score
I let the employee do most of the talking.	
I make an effort to listen to the employee's ideas.	
I am prepared to suggest solutions to the employee.	
My evaluation comments are performance-based.	
I focus and re-enforce the positive.	
I try to support and encourage the employee's ideas.	
I invite alternatives and don't assume there is only one path.	
I use open-ended questions to stimulate discussion.	
I am specific when I'm concerned about performance.	
My employees know I want them to succeed.	
I like being responsible for leading team productivity.	
I like people and enjoy talking with them.	
I don't mind giving constructive criticism.	
I provide praise freely and often when earned.	
Workers who tell me what they think don't intimidate me.	
I seek and use new ideas whenever possible.	
I respect the skills and knowledge of my employees.	
I follow up on commitments and goals that were set.	
I am sensitive to the needs and feelings of others.	
I'm not worried if employees know more than I do.	
Total	

Interpretation:

A score between 180 and 200 indicates you should be very successful in conducting performance appraisals. Scores between 140 and 179 indicate significant strength, but indicate a need for a few improvements. A score between 100 and 139 reflects some strength, but a significant number of problem areas as well. Scores below 100 call for a serious effort to improve in several categories. Make a special effort to grow in any area where you scored 6 or less, regardless of your total score.

Talking through performance problems

This tool guides you through a conversational approach to resolve performance problems with an employee. It is based on a simple decision tree model, using a tool that provides a series of 10 questions that elicit yes or no responses. The responses received from the employee trigger a specific action or a follow-up question.

Table 7. Talking through performance issues.

Questions (If Yes Response, move on to the next question)	If "No" Response
Is employee aware of their job duties?	Tell employee what to do.
Is employee aware of their performance?	Arrange for performance feedback.
Is employee aware of performance standards?	Explain performance standards.
Does employee see a need to improve?	Explain impact their performance has on company success and obtain commitment for future improvement.
Does employee have necessary skills and knowledge to do the job as expected?	Provide needed training and development.
Questions (If "No" Response... move on to next question below)	**If "Yes" Response**
Does the job appear to be too complex or big for the employee?	Consider reassignment, dividing some of the duties or provide additional training.
Does employee lack tools, equipment, materials, funds, support staff or other resources?	Provide needed resources.
Is the employee's poor work being rewarded?	Eliminate the inappropriate re-enforcers and only reward positive behaviors.
Is the employee's good work being punished or is there peer pressure against good work?	Eliminate the source of punishment and reinforce the positive behaviors.
Is the employee apathetic, negative or unconcerned?	Increase employee's level of motivation and commitment by coaching them. If this does not work use positive discipline.
If you have been through the first 10 steps without satisfaction, the final step is to restate your performance expectations and provide the opportunity for the employee to improve. If you are still not getting the desired results then both parties should "face the facts" that this might not be the best fit for the employee or employer and the person should be encouraged to seek more suitable employment opportunities elsewhere.	

Source: Robert F. Mager & Peter Pip

Strategic Talent Management

Nothing propels people towards peak performance like having their efforts noticed, appreciated, and rewarded. Wise leaders understand and accept that people have shortcomings. However, they choose to focus on their people's strengths. One example of this is attitude. If you consider the necessary elements required to be successful at any job, you will note that it takes a combination of competencies and attitude.

Skills and knowledge together equal the person's ability to do the job. But just having the ability to do the job isn't enough to guarantee peak performance. An employee's attitude accounts for 85% of their success.

Attitude is closely linked to an employee's level of motivation. A lot of leaders feel that it is their responsibility to motivate their teams. In fact, it's impossible to motivate another human being. However, the person can be enticed to make changes themselves. But when push comes to shove, the onus has to be on the individual to make the decision to change; they must motivate themselves.

Remember the old saying, "You can take a horse to water, but you can't make him drink?" In fact, you can walk the horse over to the water and say "Hey, horse, look outside, isn't that a hot day? Don't you feel hot? Aren't you thirsty? Look at that beautiful creek. Doesn't that water look great? Of course it does. Here, let me show you how good it is, and get down and actually drink the water." Now even after doing all that, if the horse decides that he's not going to drink, he's not going to drink. There's nothing you can do to force him to drink. People are very similar.

What you can do as a leader is to create an environment that makes it easier for your people to make the right decisions. In other words, create a motivating environment. If you also have the expectation that it's up to you to change and motivate your staff, then you're going to set yourself up for failure and disappointments.

Michael LeBoeuf, author of The Greatest Management Principle in the World, said, "The things that get rewarded get done; the key is to reward the right behaviors." Some of the most powerful rewards are not monetary. Rather, they are simple, tangible items that propel ordinary people to accomplish extraordinary things. The main point to remember is that it's not so much the reward that counts; it's what the reward represents. I have seen rational adults scramble to win a $10 T-shirt because it was public proof that they accomplished a goal for which they wanted recognition.

Strategic Talent Management

The best thing to do is to recognize and reward the top 20% of your people in a high-energy, entertaining, public forum surrounded by their teammates. There are literally hundreds of ideas for rewards. The key is to have fun and be creative. Feel free to ask your people for reward suggestions. The following is a small list of possible rewards:

- T-shirts/sweat shirts
- Ball caps
- Plaques/trophies/medals
- Corporate rings/watches/pens
- Certificates of accomplishment
- Gift baskets
- Bottle of fine wine/champagne
- Briefcase or portfolio with corporate name
- Gift certificate for a restaurant or a store
- Trip for two
- Certificate for a day at the spa
- Personal development book/DVD
- Crystal/figurines/sculptures
- Dinner for two
- Tickets to music concert or sporting event
- Motivational prints
- iPad

TM Solution: Reconnecting with Customers

Case study: Mid-sized European bank.
Problem/ Profit Opportunity: Disconnection with retail consumers due to "self-service models" (ATM, Internet, & telebanking).
Resources wasted: Bank felt adoption of its new revolving line of credit product was not meeting targeted usage rates. Target had been 10,000 new credit line holders with outstanding balance of €17.5 million. Results were 3,862 holders with a balance of €6.9 million. The poor results were around €510,000 less in profits.
Opportunity for a Solution: To train tellers in all bank retail locations to promote credit products after handling client transactions, and provide bonus points to each teller who referred a client to a loans officer. Points were accumulated and then cashed in for various merchandise.
Financial investment required: Creation of teller training program, rollout of training, management of points rewards program, and budget for purchasing rewards: €198,500.
Improvement generated: After one year 19,120 credit line holders, outstanding balance of €37.8 million, profits increase of €896,000.
Tracked ROI: 4.5:1

Employee rewards and recognition program

Look up the words *recognize* or *recognition* in any dictionary and you will find definitions that use words like "see," "identify," and "acknowledge". These words are at the core of what effective employee recognition is about. It's management caring enough to take the time to see, identify, and acknowledge the organizational contributions, valued behaviors, and good efforts of employees.

Recognition is an essential element to any working relationship. Employees must know that their work matters and is important to the company. As individuals, not all people value the same recognition for similar activities or behaviors. Personalizing the recognition process is the most effective way to motivate and increase performance, develop employee skills, acknowledge contributions, and meet organizational objectives.

Strategic Talent Management

Developing a rewards and recognition culture

One of the best ways to keep your people engaged is to develop a rewards and recognition culture. Rewarding talent does not have to cost a lot of money. All it takes is a bit of creativity and innovation tailored to the needs of your staff.

Below is a tool to help you develop a rewards and recognition culture. The tool has two parts. The first, a quick self-check to see how well you are developing a rewards and recognition culture within your company. The second part provides low cost/high impact ways to reward your people.

Directions: Read each question and answer: never, occasionally, or regularly.

Do you...	Never	Occasionally	Regularly
Find that staff values the rewards?			
Differentiate between top and average performers?			
Match rewards with specific needs of employers?			
Reward top performers with new opportunities?			
Recognize small improvements in poor performers?			
Reward behavior that supports company goals?			
Offer rewards based on measurable results?			
Seek input on what rewards would motivate employees?			
Communicate what is needed in order to earn rewards?			
Help employees overcome obstacles to success?			
Create a friendly competitive atmosphere among staff?			
Recognize both positive behaviors and results?			
Reward people in a way that they value?			
Say thank you for routine work and small improvements?			
Say thank you to your boss and peers?			
Offer specific examples when praising an employee?			
Enrich employees' jobs to make them more interesting?			
Reward team members equally for team results?			
Reward solving problems rather than hiding them?			
Help employees achieve work–life balance?			

Strategic Talent Management

By doing the following activities on a regular basis, you will be on the fast track to developing a rewards and recognition culture.

Seven simple steps to rewarding and recognizing employees:

1. Consider how you might like to be thanked for your efforts.
2. Ask employees what type of reward they would appreciate.
3. Praise publicly and criticize privately.
4. Develop a habit of looking for reasons to praise people (it will raise the bar).
5. Identify specific positive behavior or performance.
6. Reward/recognize the positive as soon as possible to reinforce behavior.
7. Make the process fun and engaging.

In today's society of instant gratification, employees seek frequent feedback. The notion of only discussing performance during the annual appraisal meeting is a thing of the past.

The greatest motivational myth is that money is the only motivator for workers. The following tool will help you gain insights and learn what motivates your individual workers, and what their perception is and how often they experience these on-the-job motivators.

Strategic Talent Management

Survey of individual motivators

Please read the sentences below and circle the number that tells us how important these things are to you:

	Not	Sort of	Quite	Very
Being thanked by your supervisor	0	1	2	3
Praise in front of the people you work with	0	1	2	3
Being praised on company's social media.	0	1	2	3
Interview of you and your work on YouTube	0	1	2	3
A certificate that proves you have done a good job	0	1	2	3
Getting thanked for my attendance at work	0	1	2	3
A thank you letter from the company	0	1	2	3
Getting a company award	0	1	2	3
Being thanked in the company newsletter	0	1	2	3
Getting cash for doing a good job	0	1	2	3
An ITunes gift card when you do a good job	0	1	2	3
Getting tickets to go to a special event	0	1	2	3
Getting a "years-of-service" award	0	1	2	3
Being named employee-of-the-month	0	1	2	3

Please read the sentences below and circle the number that tells us how often these things happened for you:

	Never Happened	Sometimes Happened	Often Happened
Being thanked by your supervisor	0	1	2
Being told you do a good job in front of other employees	0	1	2
Getting a certificate that proves you have done a good job	0	1	2
Getting thanked for your attendance at work	0	1	2
Getting a thank you letter from the company for doing a good job	0	1	2
Getting a company award	0	1	2
Being thanked in the company newsletter	0	1	2
Getting cash for doing a good job	0	1	2
Getting a pre-paid card when you do a good job	0	1	2
Getting tickets for a special event	0	1	2
Getting a "years-of-service" award	0	1	2
Being named employee-of-the-month	0	1	2
Being thanked by your supervisor	0	1	2

Strategic Talent Management

Challenging and Interesting Work that Develops Mastery

Onboarding: the fast-track towards mastery

Approximately one in five people in the United States and Canada will quit their job or be fired this year. This means an average of 90,000 people will be starting a new position each business day this year. The main reasons people change jobs is that they were never made to feel welcome as a part of the team when they joined.

Another big issue is that many people get hired having only a vague notion of what performance is expected of them. As a result, the new recruit never really feels connected with the company, and his/her original high level of enthusiasm soon drops to a level of apathy. Once this happens, the company will quickly fire the individual to "cut its losses." Or the person, feeling it is a useless struggle, decides to quit his job and try his luck elsewhere. Once this happens, the company they just left is once again confronted with the need to find, hire, and train someone else.

The role of effective orientation is to help the new recruit become productive as quickly as possible while maintaining the person's initial level of interest and enthusiasm. Although orientation costs time and money, for most organizations these costs are sound investments. Newly hired recruits are seldom capable of fully performing their job duties right away. Even individuals with experience need to learn about the organization — its people, its policies, and its procedures. They may need training in order to perform successfully. The gap between the new recruit's abilities and the job's demands can be substantial. A new recruit's orientation program can reduce turnover and save an organization thousands of dollars and hundreds of hours of putting out fires.

Whether a company has two team members or 20,000, the orientation of new recruits should never be left to chance. A thorough, well-planned, effectively executed orientation is an integral part of keeping your team productive and happy.

Benefits of new recruit orientation

Helps keep new recruits happy by making them feel:

- At ease and welcomed
- Good about the company
- Comfortable with their decision

Helps keep new recruits productive by:

Strategic Talent Management

- Explaining standards of performance
- Teaching basics
- Being a starting point for training and development
- Reducing mistakes and saving time
- Reducing turnover

Most new recruits start off with a great deal of energy, enthusiasm, and excitement. They are eager to prove to the company that they were a good hiring decision. The atmosphere created during the orientation program can greatly affect what happens to this person's level of interest. A quality orientation helps the recruit feel good about the opportunity. With the new recruit feeling at ease and welcomed, his/her decision to join the company will be positively reinforced. In a nutshell, the biggest benefit of orientation is the happiness the team feels.

The second major benefit of orientation is an increase in productivity. Ken Blanchard, in his book *The One Minute Manager,* talks of how he believes in passing out the final exam on the first day of his class. Blanchard does this because he wants his students to understand right from day one what performance standards are expected. By spelling out what is expected, you reduce stress that is caused by role ambiguity, and recruits can focus on important activities. The net result is lower stressed, task-driven, and highly productive people.

New recruit orientation is not difficult, and it doesn't take a lot of time if done right. A poorly planned or non-existent orientation can quickly undo all your previous recruiting and selection efforts, as one more person travels through the "revolving door" of personnel. Turnover can be greatly reduced by a well-thought-out orientation program. The results will be fewer mistakes and a better understanding of what is expected. This should lead to improved customer service, higher productivity, and improved team morale.

Everyone wins — you, the recruit, and the organization, and most of all the real bosses of any company: your customers or clients. Given human nature, we often tend to imitate what we have experienced. If you received a good orientation in the past, chances are you will conduct the program you run in a similar manner. Similarly, if your orientation was poor, then this chapter can help you develop a positive orientation program.

Strategic Talent Management

How well have you done in the past?

Think for a moment about the last few recruits your organization hired, and then honestly answer the questions on the following page.

Employee name: _____

1. How long has this person been on board?
2. Was the new recruit made to feel welcome?
3. Do you think the recruit regrets the decision to join your organization?
4. Was the person productive within a short period of time?
5. Did your organization have a planned orientation program?
6. If you had been in the recruit's place, would you have been satisfied with the orientation?
7. Did you routinely take time to get to know the recruit?
8. Did your company have a new recruit handbook, which was kept up-to-date?
9. Were welcoming events scheduled to help new recruits get acquainted?
10. Was publicity about the new recruit circulated?
11. Did new recruits have the opportunity to ask questions when they didn't understand something?

Planning the orientation program

By failing to plan, you are planning to fail. This old adage relates to many business applications, but holds especially true for orientation programs. This section will cover four key areas to ensure that your orientation program is successful. They are:

1. Reinforce the opportunity decision.
2. Make them feel welcome.
3. Start training.
4. Commit to a 90-day plan.

1. Reinforce the opportunity decision

Orientation is a great way to give the new recruits confirmation in their own mind that they have made a wise choice by accepting a position in your organization. Most likely, your new recruit could have applied for other opportunities besides this one. To reduce the incidence of "buyer's remorse" (new recruits second-guessing their decision), you can use the orientation period to reinforce the opportunity decision.

Strategic Talent Management

2. Make them feel welcome

How would you treat a client who was considering buying $15,000 of goods from your organization? Chances are you would treat them like royalty. New recruits are equally important. Set a positive first impression: roll out the red carpet. Here is a good question: Why is it that most companies reward people who leave by giving "going away" parties, but are neutral when new recruits come on board? Would it not be more beneficial to celebrate the arrival of new recruits? An easy way to provide such a welcome is to designate a room and time to invite team members to meet the new person and enjoy coffee and doughnuts.

Publicizing the hiring decision is another way to make the recruit feel welcome. There are two main ways to publicize a hiring decision: internal and external. Internally, an announcement memo could be sent to all team members, or an article could be posted on the company website. External publicity can be in the form of a press release with a photo in the business section of the local newspaper or trade journals. It is important that your organization convey to your new recruit that you are pleased they joined the organization.

It is also a good idea to remind new hires that help is available, and any questions or concerns they might have will be dealt with. Do everything in your power to ensure that new employees feel welcome.

3. Start training

Orientation provides an opportunity to start the new person on the right track. A well-planned orientation program will set the stage for all training and development that follows. During the orientation process, the skills needed to perform the basic job can be taught. Without the benefit of a progressive orientation, the recruit is left on his own to figure things out. This method is impersonal and time-consuming, as well as inefficient. New recruits lacking essential information or receiving incorrect or misleading information can learn/develop bad habits. When giving proper direction, clear tasks, and specific information, it sets the stage and a new recruit will be more receptive to training, making fewer costly errors.

4.   Commit to a 90-day plan

Everyone should want the new recruit to succeed, so it's in the best interest of all parties for you to invest a bit of time developing a 90-day plan for the new recruit.. Generally speaking, people find it hard to focus on key tasks and goals beyond 90 days, so why not plan the recruit's development and performance in a series of 90-day plans? As the first 90-day plan draws to an end, both you and the recruit should discuss the performance of the first 90 days, then set new learning, development, and performance targets and incorporate those into the second 90-day plan. One of the great benefits of having a leader/supervisor coach the new recruit is that the leader can share his experience. The recruit can quickly capitalize on the 20/80 principle (that 20% of a person's tasks or duties normally account for 80% of the value of the position).

Strategic Talent Management

TM Solution: Training from the Ground Floor

Case study: Large meat processing plant.

Problem/ Profit Opportunity: Huge staff turnover on production floor.

Resources wasted: Employee turnover of production staff was 68% for previous year. 68% turnover of 800 production workers equaled recruiting, selecting, and training 544 new people at a cost of $2,440 per new employee ($1,327,360 direct costs total).

Opportunity for a Solution: Consultant conducted surveys, exit interviews, and focus groups to discover that 95% of all turnover happened within first 30 days on the job. Morale on the production lines was poor due to the supervisors' style of managing (all supervisors had been promoted strictly due to seniority). A comprehensive new employee on-boarding program was created to make new hires feel totally welcomed and properly trained. Also, a new method of assessing potential supervisors was created, as well as a supervisor-training course.

Financial investment required: Cost of consultant: $60,000, cost of training program $22,000, internal admin cost: $10,000. Total costs: $92,000.

Improvement generated: Employee turnover reduced to 11% (88 people x $2,440 = $214,720). Net savings to company: $1,112,640.

Tracked ROI: 12:1.

Strategic Talent Management

Developing Your Key Resource: Your People

> **To do right is wonderful. To teach others to do right is even more wonderful—and much easier.**
>
> Mark Twain

One of the biggest reasons most organizations can't seem to retain great people is because they are not fully tapping into their potential. Most organizations will say this is not true, that they have dedicated training departments and training officers. It is a step in the right direction, but not enough. Great people have an overwhelming desire to become masters in their chosen field. They are very committed and will work hard to succeed. However, it's virtually impossible to succeed alone. These people crave a work environment that fosters their ongoing development. One way to see the difference is to consider the Funk & Wagnalls Dictionary definitions of two words, which are commonly treated as meaning the same thing:

- **Train:** To render qualified or obedient by instruction or drill.
- **Develop:** To expand or bring out the potential.

Most companies focus on "training" their people to "do" things better, whereas the most progressive organizations "develop" their people to "be" better. I want to be clear that I am not against training. In fact, there can be a tremendous value in increasing one's skills and knowledge base. What I am saying is that development is more holistic in nature in that it aims to help the individual realize his full potential.

Developing your people is to help them achieve their potential, while equipping them to provide the maximum benefit to the organization. In order for team development to happen, you need two key elements:

a leader who will act as a mentor while creating a positive learning environment, and an individual who is "coachable". A coachable person is someone who is enthusiastic about developing him or herself and is open to learning new things.

TM Solution: Improving the sales team

Case study: Small software company

Problem/ Profit Opportunity: Total sales of company were much less than industry average of similar-sized firms.

Resources wasted: Sales target had been $5 million @ 20% profit margin. Actual sales were $2.1 million @ 7% profit margin. Total cost of problem: $853,000.

Opportunity for a Solution: The solution was to first assess the current sales team of one manager and 10 representatives, using a sales success evaluation process. The test uncovered that the team overall lacked proficiency in several core selling competencies, the greatest one being targeting of prospects. In the past, the sales team would prospect any potential commercial account without first assessing its potential. A customized sales training program was created and delivered, and the sales manager received coaching to further develop his skills. A prospecting ABC formula was developed, and only prospects who were assessed as potentials would be sought out.

Financial investment required: Consulting, coaching and training fees: $56,000, internal costs: $10,000, total cost of solution: $66,000.

Improvement generated: After one year, sales were $12.8 million @ $2.04 million profit, less previous year's profit: $147,000 = net gain of $1.9 million.

Tracked ROI: 28.7:1

Strategic Talent Management

Individual development plans

The most straightforward development exercise is often made overly complicated: the creation of a Personal Development Plan. In fact, it is quite simple. The first step is to review the Job Description to make sure it is aligned with the direction of the organization and its strategic objectives. An up-to-date job description will lay out the related position responsibilities and the core competencies. It will also identify the desired personal characteristics of the ideal jobholder. A cautionary note— do not be too dogmatic in spelling out the exact how and when the job is to be done, if your goal is to create an agile workforce.

The second step is to fully assess the jobholder using the blank Individual Development Plan provided below. The key is to prioritize the specific areas of development and identify the sources of development. This process works best when both the leader and the jobholder jointly fill in and commit to the plan. You want to link the fulfillment of the person's dreams and aspirations with the objectives of the organization. To further illustrate the point, I have included a sample Individual Development Plan for a Sales Professional.

Sample personal development plan – Sales Professional

Developmental priorities

- Maintaining a positive outlook
- Setting meaningful goals
- Learning the power of visualization
- Effective targeting
- Relationship and rapport building
- Prospecting clients
- Powerful sales presentations
- Effective communications
- Stress management
- Time Management
- Great openers
- Uncovering buying motivators
- Handling areas of concern

Strategic Talent Management

- Telephone sales power
- Obtaining client referrals
- Networking
- Maintaining a positive attitude
- Professionalism/dress
- Finalizing the transaction
- Collecting the payment
- After-sale account building

Possible sources of development

- **On-the-job** – The most common form of training and development. In a nutshell, it means learning while performing.
- **Mentorship** – Similar to coaching, except the mentor also shares a form of relationship with the learner. More about this on the following page.
- **Company training programs** – The value of "in-house" company training programs is two-fold: the company can ensure a standardized method of sharing the same message to everyone on the team, and often no one understands the uniqueness of the company better than itself.
- **Corporate retreats/meetings** – One of the most effective development tools is to have ongoing team meetings. These meetings provide an excellent opportunity to share new ideas, products, or services with the team. By having an upbeat meeting, it will motivate everyone in attendance. Leaders should share their insights with the group so that others can learn from their experiences. Top producers and innovators should be publicly recognized and rewarded for their achievements. This encourages the entire team to strive for better results.

Strategic Talent Management

- **External seminars, workshops, and conferences** – There are numerous seminars, workshops, and conferences going on at any given time in most large cities around the planet. They can be offered by associations, chambers of commerce, universities and institutes, as well as by private seminar companies. Some are open to the public, while others are exclusive to members. The presenters can be consultants, university professors, successful local business leaders, or internationally acclaimed authors, speaking on a wide variety of topics. Some presenters also offer customized workshops tailored to the specific needs of the client.

- **Podcasts, webinars, CDs, videos, audiotapes and books** – One of the best ideas is to invest in your own development at your own pace. Podcasts, webinars, TedTalks, CDs, videos, audiotapes and books are the best sources for low-cost self-development programs. You can buy these products at bookstores, on training company websites, or you can borrow them from public libraries, boards of trade, university libraries, or the company-training department.

Cross-Training

One of the most dangerous talent situations to be in is to have one or more critical positions with only one competent person to do the job. Should something happen to that person or he decides to leave your business, without building talent redundancies, you are making your business vulnerable. It's essential to cross-train your employees to mitigate risk by developing your team's capacity.

Investing in cross-training increases the agility of your team so you can respond to fluctuating workflows. It can also include training for different skill sets in the event that a key employee leaves, while preparing a lower-level employee to move up in the organization. Cross-training provides the added benefit of giving employees a chance to build new relationships with people they might otherwise never have contact with. These relationships will help your team work more effectively and increase employees' understanding of the big picture.

Four Tips for Successful Cross-Training

Chris Cancialosi, Ph.D. offers the following tips for implementing cross training:

1. Create a culture of collective success. Some employees pride themselves on being indispensable. Make it clear that your organization values people's ability to support each other and that single points of failure are a company-wide weakness. Show employees that their capacity to help their co-workers in times of need will benefit them when they need additional support

2. Set formal expectations. Require employees to have at least one person who can step into their role at a moment's notice. Make it mandatory, give clear instructions, and provide time for people to cross-train effectively.

3. Test your success. See if a key employee can go away on vacation with absolutely no team contact, or commit that employee to another project, and make sure he isn't pulled in to help the person performing his role. If someone else is able to step into this person's absence, you're covered.

4. Develop a feedback mechanism. Give employees an opportunity to give you feedback on the impact of cross-training activities, and use this information to continuously improve your efforts.

Trusting Relationships

Companies that have mentoring programs enjoy greater productivity in the workplace. As employees turn to their mentors for advice, they make fewer mistakes on the job, cutting losses to the employer. Employees in mentoring relationships tend to have greater job satisfaction as well, which can mean a more positive work environment resulting in less employee turnover as workers feel a greater loyalty to the company. Mentoring programs also attract greater quantity and quality job applicants.

Strategic Talent Management

A mentor cares about the mentee's long-term success and commits to help in the "fast-tracking" of the person's development. This is done by the mentor sharing lessons he has learned over the years. This form of compressed learning can shave off many years of learning for the mentee.

> **The number one reason most people leave a good paying job is not the nature of the work, rather it is the nature of the person they have to work with.**
>
> Gallop

⚠ Can one bad apple really spoil the whole bunch?

Cornerstone Research recently studied 63,000 employees regarding the impact of "toxic employees" in the workplace. Key report findings included:

- Top performers are 54% more likely to quit when they work with a toxic employee. That proportion grows if the number of toxic employees in a company reaches as little as one in a team of 20.

- Toxic employees make their co-workers significantly more likely to leave, and replacement costs rise by hiring even one toxic employee into a team of 20 workers. That single toxic employee raises costs by approximately $12,800, whereas hiring a non-toxic employee costs an employer an average of $4,000.

- Toxic employees can negatively affect the performance of their co-workers, and they can create stress and burnout within colleagues.

Strategic Talent Management

Mentoring- and Coaching-Based Performance Improvement

These five steps will improve performance using a mentoring/coaching approach:

1. Create a relationship with your mentee.
   - Identify any personal emotional triggers or listening blocks that would interfere with your effective listening.
   - Find a right time to raise the issue.
   - Demonstrate genuine interest and belief in the mentee.
   - Use an inviting and encouraging tone of voice.

2. Present the performance issue.
   - Start by reinforcing a positive by pointing out a specific accomplishment or success. Remember the Sandwich Technique.
   - Be clear and direct about what the performance redirection issue is.
   - Limit the statement to a single issue (not a whole litany).
   - Use objective language, free of blame or judgment.
   - Emphasize the wish to resolve the issue (redirect behavior) positively.
   - Indicate belief in the mentee's abilities, including his or her ability to resolve issues.

3. Listen for the mentee's perspective.
   - Put aside your own agenda while listening.
   - Listen actively to understand the mentee's perspective. Remember the "ask vs. tell" 30/70 approach.
   - Paraphrase and use open-ended clarifying questions.
   - Acknowledge the mentee's perspective.

4. Resolve the issue with the worker.
   - Maintain a focus on work-related behaviors.
   - Reach mutual agreement on the nature of the problem.
   - Develop strategies together to address the problem.
   - Move towards wrapping up by reinforcing a positive, pointing out a specific accomplishment or success. Remember the second bun in the Sandwich.

Strategic Talent Management

5. Get commitment to action steps.
   - Make mutual commitments for specific, measurable action steps.
   - Follow through on commitments.

Mentoring and coaching self-check

Every job where you supervise people, or have people reporting to you is a "mentoring or coaching" role. Each supervisor should fill out the following self-check tool. The business owner could discuss with their business partner, spouse, or another business owner. The purpose of these discussions is to focus on areas of personal development.

Directions: Read each statement and score on a scale of 1 (totally inaccurate) to 10 (very accurate). The higher the number, the more the statement reflects you. Then add up the total of all of your scores.

Statements	Score
I promote teamwork and discourage "us versus them" thinking.	
I provide clear directions on how the job should be done.	
I set the example of how my team should work together.	
I create an environment where people feel respected, valued, and appreciated.	
I encourage the giving and receiving of feedback.	
I help employees focus on key activities that contribute to our company success.	
I create an environment focused on productivity.	
I clearly communicate company goals so everyone can contribute to them.	
I set clear expectations and let people know how well they are meeting them.	
I set high standards for my performance and encourage others to do the same.	
I involve my people in making decisions.	
I encourage and reward creativity and innovation.	
I encourage people to stretch beyond their current abilities.	
I praise people publicly and I criticize privately.	
I model enthusiasm and loyalty to the company and the brand.	
I help people take ownership of results by holding them accountable.	
Total	

Interpretation:

A score between 140 and 160 indicates you should be a very successful mentor/ coach. Scores between 120 and 140 indicate significant strength, plus a few improvements needs. A score between 90 and 120 reflects some strength, but a significant number of problem areas to work on. Scores below 90 call for a serious effort to improve in several categories. Make a special effort to grow in any area where you scored 6 or less, regardless of your total score.

Salary, Benefits and Bonuses

In the movie, *Jerry Maguire*, Tom Cruise's character often uttered the catch phase, "Show me the money." It's a common misconception that money is considered the biggest motivator for all people. Yes, some people are money motivated, if fact some are very much so. However, to lump everyone into this category is incorrect at best and downright dangerous in most cases. Yes, people need to work for money, having all sorts of financial obligations to meet. To that end, a lack of competitive pay is demotivating to talent, as their primary needs are not being met. If this is the case, people will jump ship for higher pay even if there are beanbag chairs and a Foosball machine in the lunch area. If employers want to attract and retain talent, they must offer a competitive pay package. I recommend paying 75% to 85% relative to what work of similar value is being offered in your geographic area. The resources, left over by not being the "highest bidder" will allow you to afford many creative low cost/ high impact ideas that were previously mentioned in appreciation, recognition and rewards section of this chapter.

Incentive Pay and Other Compensation Plans

> **If people relate to the company they work for, if they form an emotional tie to it and buy into its dreams, they will pour their heart into making it better.**
>
> Howard Schultz

Strategic Talent Management

Tap into employee creativity

A fantastic way to not only engage your staff but also uncover practical methods of improving operations, cutting costs, and/or increasing sales is to tap into the creative minds of your talent. Your employees will often see things differently than your senior managers, so it makes sense to tap into their creativity while also creating a culture that fosters the mindset that every employee's opinions and creative suggestions are valued and highly encouraged.

Net gain program template – Employee suggestions

As employees of our company, you have the opportunity to contribute to our future success and growth by submitting suggestions for practical work   improvement or cost   savings ideas. All employees are eligible to participate in the suggestion program.

A suggestion is an idea that will benefit our company by solving a problem, reducing costs, improving operations or procedures, enhancing customer service, eliminating waste or spoilage, or making our company a better or safer place to work. Statements of problems without accompanying solutions, or recommendations concerning co workers and management, are not appropriate suggestions.

All suggestions should contain a description of the problem or condition to be improved, a detailed explanation of the solution or improvement, and the reasons why it should be implemented. If you have questions or need advice about your idea, contact your supervisor for help.

Submit suggestions in the appropriate Suggestion Box, and these will be passed on for review on a monthly basis. As soon as possible, you will be notified of the adoption or rejection of your suggestion. A suggestion bonus will be paid to every suggestion that is implemented. The size of this bonus will depend on the net gain to the company.

Strategic Talent Management

Net gain suggestion form

Directions:

- Complete this form and attach any relevant diagrams, sketches, photos, or other information to fully communicate your net gain suggestion.
- Sign and date the form and submit to HR.

Present situation: Describe the present situation, method, procedure or service (describe what is done now, by whom, when and how it is done).

_____

_____

Proposed net gain suggestion: Describe your suggestion for changing or improving the present situation, method, procedure or service (include the areas that would be affected by the change, and an estimation of the costs of implementing your suggestion).

_____

_____

Benefit to the company: Describe the benefit(s) of your net gain suggestion. Include the cost savings and/or the increase in sales intended by your suggestion.

_____

_____

Is there someone else familiar with this situation who might help evaluate and or implement your suggestion?

If yes, please provide name: _____ Title: _____

Telephone: _____ Email: _____

Name of person making suggestion: _____

Title: _____

Department: _____ Employee #: _____

Signature: _____ Date: _____

Strategic Talent Management

Wellness and Safety Programs
TM Solution: Wellness pay

Case study: Mid-sized food distribution company.
Problem/ Profit Opportunity: Employees taking too many sick days.
Resources wasted: Almost all 80 warehouse and delivery staff claimed their allotted 10 days of sick leave per year. Average cost per employee per year was $1,200 x 80 employees = $96,000 plus $44,000 in overtime and management time to cover absent staff. Total cost (not factoring in several clients who were disgruntled due to lapses in deliveries): $140,000.
Opportunity for a Solution: Pay wellness cash bonus to all staff with perfect attendance.
Financial investment required: Cash bonus of $250 per qualified employee. Supervisors and management exempt.
Improvement generated: 68 employees awarded bonus in first year resulted in cost of program: 68 x $250 = $17,000, plus program set-up and admin cost: $2,000, total cost year one = $19,000. Saved costs of 68 x $1,200 = $81,600.
Tracked ROI: 4.3:1.

Strategic Talent Management

TM Solution: Safety Equipment Account

Case study: Large industrial construction company.

Problem/ Profit Opportunity: Company felt it was spending too much on personal safety equipment.

Resources wasted: With around 2,000 employees, the company decided to bulk buy safety boots, hard hats, safety glasses, and work gloves, and provide two free replacement sets to each worker. Annual cost: $540 per employee x 2,000 employees = $1,080,000.

Opportunity for a Solution: Given that historically, gloves only lasted about half a year, the company continued to provide two sets per year. However, it was discovered that in many cases the other safety equipment lasted much longer. Each employee was provided a budget of $300 per year to obtain safety gear. If they abused their gear, they would have to top up the difference. If they took care of their gear (and it passed the twice yearly safety inspections), they would get the remaining balance of their budget to keep for themselves.

Financial investment required: Set up and admin program: $5,000 plus $340 x 2,000 = $685,000.

Improvement generated: $395,000.

Tracked ROI: 1.7:1.

TM Solution: Accident reduction and safety program

Case study: Large Caribbean rum distiller.

Problem/ Profit Opportunity: Accidents among 500 production workers were on the rise, costing the company in terms of money and damage to its reputation.

Resources wasted: Forty-eight accidents the prior year totaled $723,000 (includes medical care costs, disability payments, admin costs, and one legal settlement).

Opportunity for a Solution: Zero accident training and awards program.

Financial investment required: Set up and administrate training and awards program: $20,000, paying out of Zero Accident awards per employee for each three-month period accident-free: $150 = $299,700, total program costs: $319,700.

Improvement generated: First year saw two accidents, with a total cost of $12,900. Net reduction of accident-related costs: $710,100 (not to mention the goodwill associated with becoming one of the safest employers).

Tracked ROI: 2.2:1.

> No one cares how much you know, until they know how much you care!
>
> Cavett Roberts

Strategic Talent Management

A simple yet powerful way to understand total employee recognition is CARES:

- **C**ompensation
- **A**ssistance and benefits
- **R**ecognition and rewards
- **E**qual work–life balance
- **S**ystem of personal and professional development

Note: If you do not provide most of these elements for your employees, compensation will by default become the primary motivator. When this happens, the highest bidding company wins.

CARES Elements Definitions

- Compensation: Pay provided by an employer to an employee for services rendered.
- Assistance and benefits: Programs an employer uses to supplement the cash compensation that employees receive. These health, income protection, savings, and retirement assistance programs provide security for employees and their families.
- Recognition and rewards: Acknowledges employee actions, efforts, behavior or performance. Fulfills employees' need for appreciation of their efforts and supports business strategy by reinforcing positive behaviors that contribute to organizational success. Awards can be cash or non-cash (verbal recognition, trophies, certificates, plaques, dinners, tickets, etc.).
- Equal work–life balance: A specific set of organizational practices, policies and programs, driven by a philosophy that actively supports employees achieving success, both at work and at home.
- System of personal and professional development: A set of learning experiences, within the employee's career plan, designed to enhance the employee's applied skills and competencies. Development helps employees perform better and engage leaders in advancing their organization's people strategies. The company supports career opportunities internally so that talented employees are deployed into positions that let them deliver their greatest value to the organization.

Strategic Talent Management

Compensation	Assistance & Benefits	Recognition & Rewards	Equal Work–Life Balance	System of Career Development
Base Wages Salary Pay Hourly Pay Piece Rate Pay **Premium Pay** Shift Differential Pay Weekend/Holiday Pay On-Call Pay Call-In Pay Hazard pay Skill-Based Pay **Variable Pay** Commissions Team-Based Pay Bonus Programs Referral Bonus Hiring Bonus Retention Bonus Project Completion Bonus Incentive Pay **Short-term** Profit Sharing Individual Performance- Based Incentives Performance-Sharing Incentives **Long-term** Restricted Stock Performance Shares Performance Units Stock Options/Grants	**Legally Mandated** Unemployment Insurance Worker's Compensation Social Security **Health & Welfare** Medical Plan Dental Plan Vision Plan Prescription Drug Plan Life Insurance Spouse/Dependent Life Insurance AD&D Insurance Short-Term/Long-Term Disability Insurance **Retirement** Company Pension Plan RSP Co-Contributions **Additional** Vacation Holiday Sick Leave Bereavement Leave Leaves of Absence (Jury Duty, Personal, Medical, Family Medical) Maternity/Paternity Leave Adoption Leave Sabbaticals	**Recognition** Service Awards Retirement Awards Peer Recognition Awards Spot Awards Managerial Recognition Programs Organization-Wide Recognition Programs Exceeding Performance Awards Employee of the Month/ Year Awards Appreciation Luncheons/ Outings Formal Events Goal-Specific Awards (Quality, Efficiency, Cost-Savings, Productivity, Safety) Employee Suggestion Programs	**Workplace Flexibility** Flex-Time Flexible Schedules Telecommuting Compressed Workweek Job Sharing Part-time Employment Seasonal Schedules **Health & Wellness** Employee Assistance On-site Fitness Facilities Fitness Club Discounts Wellness Programs On-Site Massages Immunization Clinics Health Screenings Nutritional Counseling On-Site Nurse Occupational Health Disability Management Return to Work Programs Reproductive Health/ Pregnancy Programs **Community Involvement** Community Volunteering Matching Gift Programs Shared Leave Programs Disaster Relief Funds Sponsorships/Grants In-Kind Donations **Caring for Dependents** Dependent Care Services On-Site Childcare Support Groups Adoption Assistance After-School Care College Scholarships **Financial Support** Financial Planning Services and Education Bus Transit Subsidies **Voluntary Benefits** Long-Term Care Auto/Home Insurance Legal Insurance Identity Theft Insurance Employee Discounts Bicycle Program Parking **Culture Change Initiatives** Work Redesign Team Effectiveness Diversity/Inclusion Initiatives Women's Advancement Initiatives Work Environment Initiatives	**Learning Opportunities** Tuition Reimbursement Tuition Discounts Corporate Universities New Technology Training On-the-Job Learning Outside Seminars and Conferences Virtual Learning, Podcasts, Webinars Self-Development Tools **Coaching/Mentoring** Leadership Training Access to Onsite Experts Access to Information Networks Formal or Informal Mentoring Programs **Advancement Opportunities** Internships Apprenticeships Overseas Assignments Internal Job Postings Job Advancement/ Promotion Career Ladders and Pathways Succession Planning On/Off Ramps through Career Lifecycle Job Rotations

Strategic Talent Management

Surveying the FACTS of Your Employee Engagement

For the FACTS regarding the level of your employee engagement, I created the following ready-to-use survey based on my model **The FACTS of Engaging & Retaining Exceptional People**. The following is a reminder of the five most important factors people seek in their ideal employer.

Flexibility & autonomy of work arrangements

Appreciation, recognition, rewards and frequent feedback

Challenging and Interesting work that develops mastery

Trusting relationships

Salary, benefits and bonuses

Employee Engagement Survey

The following survey is an opportunity for you to provide feedback on how you feel about working here. We strive to make our organization a place where every teammate will be both happy and productive, and we greatly appreciate your feedback as we continue to improve. The survey is 100% anonymous. All employees are highly encouraged to take a few moments to complete the survey, fold it and drop it in the cardboard box marked "Survey".

What is your gender? _____ Male _____ Female

What is your age? _____ Under 20 _____ 20 to 29_____ 30 to 39 _____ 40 to 49 _____ 50 to 59 _____ 60+

How long have you worked for our organization?

_____ Less than 1 year _____ 1 to 2 yrs _____ 2 to 3 yrs _____ 4 to 5 yrs _____ 5 to 10yrs _____10yrs +

Strategic Talent Management

Directions: Please read each sentence below and use this scale to indicate how much you agree with each statement:

1= Totally disagree	2=Somewhat disagree	3 = Neutral	4 = Somewhat agree	5 = Totally agree

Statement	1	2	3	4	5
I have the ability and flexibility to choose how, when and where I work.					
I can greatly influence my workplace environment.					
I feel appreciated for my contributions and I receive appropriate recognition and/ or rewards when my performance exceeds expectations.					
I receive ongoing informal and formal performance feedback on my strengths, as well as opportunities for development.					
I feel that my work is interesting, challenging and provides the opportunity to do what I do best every day.					
I have an individual development plan that is guiding me towards mastery in my position.					
I trust my supervisor and feel that he is honest and open with me.					
I value the professional relationships I have with my colleagues.					
My compensation is competitive with other employers in the area.					
My benefits package is comprehensive and competitive.					
Overall I am very satisfied being in my department.					
Overall I am very satisfied with my job.					
Overall I am very happy to be part of our organization.					

Please feel free to include any additional comments or suggestions below.

_____

_____

_____

_____

Thanks for sharing your feedback & suggestions

Strategic Talent Management

TM Metrics

The following are some TM Questions on the topic of engaging and retaining exceptional people you might want to consider adding to your TM Scoreboard.

- How is engagement measured and how often is it measured?

- What is the overall engagement level of the workforce and do these levels vary by country, location, department, and manager?

- Are engagement levels increasing or decreasing over time?

- How has the workplace been impacted (productivity, employee turnover, sales customer satisfaction and profits) as a result of engagement surveys?

- Are leaders held accountable for engagement levels of the workforce, and have managers been trained on ways to improve employee engagement?

- Are engagement results shared with all employees and made public?

- Are there on-going assessments and improvements being made to the on-boarding program? How has the on-boarding program impacted new employee engagement, retention, learning curve, reduction in wastage, and rework?

- How long does it take employees to become "job proficient?" How does this time to proficiency vary by recruiter, department and/ or hiring manager?

- Are individual development plans (IDPs) created for every employee? What impact has IDPs had on productivity and business results?

- Do executives serve as mentors and teach in leadership development programs?

- Do mentoring and developmental conversations between manager and employee occur frequently?

- Other possible TM questions…

Strategic Talent Management

Chapter Four: Working with Four Different Age Groups

Never before have we experienced four different demographic cohorts represented within the workforce. It is imperative that leaders understand the fundamental elements that have shaped each group, and how to best attract, engage, develop and retain them. With millennials representing 50% or more of the entire global workforce by 2020 and 75% by 2025, it behooves leaders to place a special focus on this growing segment of talent. This cohort is the most agile, tech savvy, globally-minded of the four groups. Organizations that can fully tap into the millennial workforce will own the future. The following chart is a distillation of many reports and books (Half, Mercer, Cox, Zenke, Rains and others) detailing the differences between these four demographic groups.

Veterans 1927 – 1945	Baby Boomers 1946 – 1964	Generation "X" 1965 - 1983	Millennial 1984 – 2002
Other Names			
Traditionalists, Silent, Moral Authority, Radio Babies, The Forgotten Generation	"Me" Generation, Moral Authority	Gen X, Xers, The Doer, Post Boomers, 13th Generation	Generation Y, Gen Y, Generation Next, Echo Boomers, 24/7's
Famous People			
Bob Hope, Elizabeth Taylor	Bill Clinton, Meryl Streep	Barak Obama, Jennifer Lopez	Ashton Kutcher, Taylor Swift
Major Influencers			
• Great Depression • WWI & WWII	• Vietnam War • Cold War • Feminism • Space travel • Separation church/ state	• Divorce rates • Single parent homes • Working moms • Latchkey kids • Downsizing • Y2K	• 911 • Social media • AIDS • School shootings • No losers • Helicopter parents

Strategic Talent Management

Veterans 1927 – 1945	Baby Boomers 1946 – 1964	Generation "X" 1965 - 1983	Millennial 1984 – 2002
Factors That Shaped Perspectives			
• Parents' views • Community/ religious values • Respected leaders	• Family views • Friends' values • Political events	• World events on TV • Friends' values • Family views	• Community values • Grandparents' views • World events • Internet
Factors Affecting Overall Happiness			
• Financial security • Personal health • Family happiness • Personal safety • Economic conditions	• Financial security • Job status • Community status • Family happiness • Personal health	• Family happiness • World events • Leisure time • Local politics • Job happiness	• Friendships • Leisure time • Job happiness • Environmental issues • World events
Personality Preferences			
• Consistency • Uniformity • Grand scale • Law & order • Frugality • Logic	• Teamwork • Personal gratification • Center of attention • Optimism • Expansion	• Balance • Sense of Family • Informality • Casual authority • Self-reliance	• Collective action • Optimism • Tenacity • Multi-tasking • Tech savvy
Career Goals			
Build a legacy	Build a stellar career	Build a portable career	Build parallel career
What "Balance" Means To Them			
Support me in shifting the balance	Help me balance everyone else	Give me balance now, not when I'm 65	I need flexibility so I can balance all my non-work activities

Strategic Talent Management

Veterans 1927 - 1945	Baby Boomers 1946 – 1964	Generation "X" 1965 - 1983	Millennial 1984 – 2002
What Recruiting Messages They Look For In A Company			
• Project or part-time work • Flexible benefits • Job security • Opportunity to use own experience	• Career path potential • Salary, job title/status • Tailored benefits • Learning opportunities	• "Hands off supervision" • Fun workplace • Match of company & personal values • Salary & benefits • Growth opportunities	• "We want you to have a life" • Salary • Friendly, casual work environment • Growth opportunities • Tech innovator
Orientating Them			
• Explain policies, expectations • Cover company history • Share the big-picture	• Allow them to get to work quickly • Explain future of company • Discuss possible challenges	• Focus on "dos" not "dues" • Modulized orientation • Encourage their interaction	• Want to be able to ask many questions • Likes fast-paced • Computer based
Their Retention Attitudes			
Job hopping carries a stigma	Job changing puts you behind	Job changing is necessary to build my resume	Job changing is part of my daily routine
What Keeps Them With The Same Company			
• Satisfaction of job well done • Hand written thank you • Experience/expertise is respected • Flexible benefits • Company is loyal	• Money • Job title, corner office • Advancement opportunities • Experience/expertise is respected • Interesting work	• Career development opportunities • Work/life balance • Integrity/values of company • Freedom is ultimate reward	• Ideas/input respected • Company values same as personal • Career development opportunities • Work that has meaning to them

Strategic Talent Management

Veterans 1927 - 1945	Baby Boomers 1946 – 1964	Generation "X" 1965 - 1983	Millennial 1984 – 2002
Characteristics of Other Generations That Bother Them The Most			
• Young people not respecting elders • Young people with no work ethic • Young people impatient for success	• Young people have no company loyalty • Young people with no work ethic • Young people impatient for success	• Boomers are too bossy • Veterans reject change • Gen Y have no work ethic	• Older people too bossy • Older people resist technology • Older people don't respect them
What They Want The Other Generations To Know About Them			
• My brain still works • There are good reasons to do things a certain way • I want to continue to work	• I'll be around for a long time • I am not an aging hippie • There are good reasons to do things a certain way	• I can make a contribution to society • I will not stay with a company that doesn't have integrity • I do have a good work ethic	• I want to make a difference • I expect to be treated with respect • I won't play by your rules without a good reason

DID YOU KNOW

An Employer of Choice for Millennials

A recent in-depth survey by Deloitte showed that Millennials are seeking the following attributes (by order of importance) in an employer of choice:

- Opportunities for career progression
- Mentoring and coaching from senior executives
- Competitive wages and other financial incentives
- Individualized training and development plans
- Good benefits packages
- Flexible working arrangements
- Good reputation for ethical practices
- Corporate values in line with own
- Reputation of hiring best and brightest people
- Diversity/ Equal opportunities record
- The sector in which organization operates

Strategic Talent Management

Chapter Five: TM Planning

One of the best areas to get great bottom-line results is in HR planning. At the end of the day, it's people who implement your critical business plans. It only makes sense that your company has an HR plan to make sure that the right people with the right competencies and attitudes are in the right positions, as well as the right direction, and developmental support and feedback. An HR plan puts all these elements together.

There are three key elements of HR planning that drive organizational effectiveness, and thus the bottom-line.

1. **Succession planning** – ensures the continuity of having the right people in the right jobs, especially for key and hard-to-find positions.
2. **Effective layoffs and outsourcing** – maintains a lean and keen organization.
3. **Capitalizing on technology** – streamlines the HR function.

Succession Planning

Succession planning is when you identify your long-range human resource needs and cultivate a supply of internal talent to meet those future needs. You can use succession planning to anticipate the future needs of your organization and help you find (internally and externally), assess, and develop the human capital you need for the success of your organization.

> **76% of all organizations with 500+ employees have no formal succession plan, this number increases as the number of total employees is smaller…the risk of failing to plan for the timely succession of key and hard to fill positions becomes critical with smaller organizations.**
>
> American Society of Training & Development

Benefits of Succession Planning

For the organization:

- Identifies future leaders
- Ensures you have the right people in place
- Ensures continuity of production, sales, and customer service
- Engages employees and reduces turnover
- Protects profits

For management:

- Ensures the "right person" is in the right role
- Identifies potential "risks" within the organization
- Makes it easier to effectively manage changes of key personnel

For the individual:

- Identifies skill gaps and manages development
- Motivates individuals by stretching their abilities
- Helps them understand where they currently fit within the organization

> **Succession planning and TM are the #1 issues in business today.**
>
> Economist Magazine

Seven Questions in Succession Planning

When starting succession planning, it is helpful to ask these questions:

1. How many retirements are going to hit your organization in the next few years?
2. Have you prepared for a sudden loss of your key, or hard-to-fill, positions should a worst case scenario happen (ill health, death, early retirement, leaving for other opportunity)?

3. Have you identified and trained people who are ready to fill these key or hard-to-fill positions?
4. What is your plan to fill any talent gaps?
5. Where will you find the people to fill these key or hard-to-fill positions? (Develop or hire decision)
6. What is your retention plan to engage and motivate key employees to stay and contribute?
7. Does your company have a structured and well-documented plan for succession?

> **Too Many Companies Lack All Important Succession Plans**
>
> Wall Street Journal

Common Problems in Succession Planning

Here are some of the more common problems you may come across as you begin succession planning for your organization:

- **Defining it as an HR problem.** It is actually a responsibility shared by the senior leadership team, supervisors, and even individual workers. Everyone has some responsibility to groom talent to meet the organization's future needs.

- **Under-resourcing the effort.** A good succession program requires time and effort. Someone must coordinate that. It cannot be "completely outsourced." Consultants can help, but they cannot "do it for you." Managers cannot abdicate responsibility — or accountability. It is critical to have a succession planning committee dedicated to the creation and implementation of the succession plan.

- **Establishing confused or overly ambitious goals.** If the organization's leaders do not focus the succession effort on specific and measurable objectives to be achieved, the succession program will lack goal clarity, and resources will be wasted in pursuing many confusing, overlapping, and perhaps conflicting goals. You have to be clear about what you want before a program can be established to accomplish it.

- **Failing to hold people accountable.** This is perhaps the biggest problem facing all succession programs. What happens if this year's individual development plans are not met by your employees? What happens if the supervisor in charge of a section does not meet measurable talent development objectives for his or her team? How do we arrange consequences for building talent, or failing to build talent? How does talent development stack up against meeting the numbers for this month, quarter, or year? What do we do if we are making profits or sales but not grooming people for the future?

Twelve Commandments of De-hiring Staff

1. **Sound the alarm** – Assuming the offense is not so severe that it warrants immediate dismissal, in most cases of negative behavior, sound the alarm. Give the employee a verbal warning first. For a second offense, a documented written warning. For a third, termination of employment.

    Giving employees appropriate warnings provides them with the chance to correct their negative behavior. Point out to employees where they've been falling short of expectations. Be very clear with what you expect of them, and let them know that failure to comply with these reasonable expectations will lead to termination of employment. If dismissal is inevitable, you have then established an excellent defense for a bona fide termination.

    How can you tell if an employee's problem is their attitude, or a training problem? One quick "test" you can use — and I do not mean to do this literally — is to imagine yourself pointing a gun at the head of your employees and telling them to go ahead and perform the tasks. If they immediately jump up and successfully complete the task, you know the problem has been attitudinal. They can actually do the job, but have chosen not to.

On the other hand, if an employee looks at you with fear in their eyes and replies, "Gee boss, I would really like to do that for you, but I don't know how," then what you're confronted with is a training problem. If this is the case, don't chastise them; take the time to train them. However, if you've determined that this person isn't trainable and there's nothing else for them to do within your organization, you probably have to let them go.

2. **Take your time** – Many people take days, if not weeks, to find, select, and hire the right person. Yet often, in the heat of the moment, leaders make irrational decisions and fire someone on the spot. I like to try to give as much time, thought, and energy to the firing decision as I do to the original hiring decision. Make sure you've tried every reasonable alternative to change the negative behavior first, and that you're sure dismissing the person is indeed the correct decision to make.

3. **Don't delegate the task** – If the person being dismissed works directly for you, the act of firing them is a responsibility you should never delegate. By doing so, this unpleasant task is likely to be perceived as being unfair to all concerned.

4. **The timing and location** – Although it's often been said that the best time to dismiss someone is late on Friday afternoon, I doubt that is necessarily a preferred time, given today's flexible work shifts. Also, it can come to be expected that Friday is the time that people are fired in your company. It's better to find a quiet place and a reasonable block of uninterrupted time to deal with the issue, regardless of the day.

5. **Do your homework** – You must be prepared in advance. Have all the appropriate records, forms, and employee's personnel file with you at all times; as well as any performance evaluations needed to justify your decision to dismiss this person. Always give the employee a detailed memo outlining the reasons for termination.

6. **Get to the point** – Once the meeting begins, don't drag it out: get to the point. The more you procrastinate on giving the bad news, the more difficult and uncomfortable it will be for both parties. Be tactful, direct, and sincere, but do get to the point quickly.

7. **Stick to your decision** – The dismissal interview is not the time or place to second-guess your decision, nor to act as a counseling service for the employee. Your role is to convey the message that this person's employment is being terminated, and to do so in the quickest and most tactful manner possible.

8. **Prepare yourself for the worst** – The funny thing about human nature is that there is no accurate way to predict what someone is going to do in a stressful situation. So be prepared for the worst. I've seen very tall, robust men break down and cry. I've had women threaten me, while others simply stare into space and mumble. Getting fired can be quite a shock to a person, but it shouldn't be if they've heard the warnings. The key thing is to anticipate, in advance, the worst possible scenario. Chances are it probably won't happen, but if it does, be prepared for it. Always remember to act in a professional and courteous manner. Do your best to be sympathetic and understanding.

   The best approach, I've found, when someone reacts in a shocked manner, is to allow several moments to pass for the employee to absorb and accept the news, and then try to move on. Re-focus their attention on getting their life back on track by saying something like, "Frank, I certainly hope you'll find future employment that will be more in line with your personal requirements."

9. **Be consistent** – If you give any form of support to someone leaving your organization, be consistent by giving the same type of support to everyone who leaves. There are three main types of support that can be included in a termination policy:

Strategic Talent Management

- **Financial assistance** – Above and beyond severance pay, you may include the continuation of medical and life insurance benefits.

- **Secretarial support services** – Some companies routinely provide office space and secretarial services for middle-line and upper-level managers, to help them in their job search.

- **Outplacement services** – Your company may choose to hire an independent company that specializes in helping displaced workers and executives find new employment.

10. Be careful about how your other employees will respond. It's very important that the morale of your organization does not suffer as a result of this dismissal. Whenever possible, it's important you explain to your remaining staff why the individual was fired (without being specific), and reassure them that their jobs are not in jeopardy. If unchecked, the rumor mill can start working overtime, and you may have your entire staff second-guessing their own jobs.

11. **Exit interviews** – Exit interviews should be conducted with departing employees either just before they leave, or just after they have left the company. From the employer's perspective, the main goal of the exit interview is to learn the reasons for the person's departure. Exit interviews are also an opportunity for transfer of knowledge and experience from the departing employee to a successor or replacement, or even to brief a team on current projects, issues, and contacts.

Exit interviews are best done face-to-face because it allows better communication, understanding, and interpretation of the information being passed on. It also provides a far better opportunity to probe and get to the root of sensitive or reluctant feelings. However, mailed or electronic questionnaires are better than nothing, if face-to-face exit interviews are not possible.

In terms of managing the interview, listen rather than talk. Give the interviewee time and space to answer. Keep calm, and resist the urge to defend or argue. Your aim is to elicit views, feedback, and answers, not to lecture or admonish. Obviously, the style of exit interview is different for someone who is retiring, or being asked to leave/being made redundant/ being dismissed, compared with an employee leaving for a better opportunity (who your organization would prefer to retain).

However, everyone who leaves should be given the opportunity for an exit interview, because your organization can learn something from every situation. In certain situations (where appropriate), the exit interview also provides a last chance to change a person's mind, although this should not be the main aim of the exit interview.

12. **Last Step.** When the interview is complete, say thanks and wish the interviewee well. If there is some specific follow-up to do, make sure you do it and report back accordingly. After the interview, look at the answers and think thoroughly — in a detached and objective way — about their meaning and implications.

Capitalizing On Technology

At this point in the book, I have talked about many specific areas where HR can add to the profits of your company. Any well thought-out and implemented investment of time and money in HR should yield some net gains. The challenge for most companies is that their HR function evolved over time and has become a patchwork collection of manual processes developed internally, and various external manual and software-based processes.

For example, a company could have developed most of its HR processes internally over many years with several people taking the lead. The recruiting process may be supported by an independent consultant conducting paper-based psychometric assessments. An off-the-shelf software program might do payroll. Having this type of HR system is certainly better than no system, but a non-integrated complex maze of processes stemming from various employees (some no longer with the company), and external vendors who operate independently, is far from ideal. If HR processes are segmented between various internal and external sources, there can be many drawbacks ranging from errors, gaps, and delays in reporting, to software programming conflicts.

Strategic Talent Management

As a consultant, I have seen countless clients struggling, frustrated with this patchwork reality. It's very common for me to see several job description and performance appraisal templates used in the same company. Some departments use competency-based interviews, while others just use a quick informal "gut check" interview. This patchwork approach becomes even more cumbersome and less effective as the company grows in size and complexity. In fact, the ineffectiveness of this approach to HR will eventually hamper business growth and profitability.

What is needed is an integrated holistic approach to manage the company's HR function. Given the massive gains in technology over the past decade, specifically thanks to the Internet, there are literally thousands of HR-based software programs available, many as apps for your tablet. The caution here is to be careful not to get caught up with the next flavor or fad-of-the-month app, or software that focuses on only part of the HR function.

If a client of mine is looking to invest in HR automation, I tell him to take the time and do it right by investing in what the industry refers to as Software-as-a-Service (commonly called SaaS). These types of solutions differ from traditional software solutions because they are hosted in a central cloud and delivered on-demand.

A quality HR SaaS system provides the best of both worlds, in that the company never loses control over their HR function, but they eliminate costly onsite IT equipment, maintenance, and human overhead. The benefits of an HR SaaS system is less frustration, better reporting, and improved analysis at a lower cost. The point is not to replace all of HR with machines, but to off-load high-cost transactional HR activities, while freeing up time so that HR leaders can be more strategic in the value they provide. In the area of HR SaaS, there are only a small number of serious providers who meet my criteria.

Strategic Talent Management

Criteria	Findings
Does the vendor support my specific country/region with software accommodating local labor laws?	
How user-friendly is the software? Is the dashboard customizable?	
Is the solution scalable and able to handle growth of the company?	
Is tech support available 24/7?	
Is remote access available 24/7 for users?	
Does the solution handle an integrated approach to the complete life cycle of an employee (recruitment, prescreening, interviewing, reference checking, hiring, on-boarding, pay role and benefits admin, skills inventory, learning and performance management, succession planning and exit management)?	
How long has the vendor been offering this service? Does the vendor have experience with similar sized companies? Does the vendor have clients in my industry? Does the vendor have a high client retention rate? Do they have reliable client references?	
What proof of ROI does the vendor have (specific case studies of real clients detailing ROI and investment pay-back period).	

HR in Partnership with Customer Service, Sales, and Marketing

HR has made, and continues to make great contributions in the areas of customer service, sales, and marketing. Any wise investments you make to improve the performance of the people in these critical areas will yield great returns. Below are two examples of how I have worked with different clients to create unique HR solutions to grow their businesses.

Strategic Talent Management

TM Solution: Creative Ways to Enhance Brand

Case study: Large financial services company.

Problem/ Profit Opportunity: Senior executives felt that consumers, after the recent banking crises, saw all financial companies as great sources of corporate greed, all too willing to seek taxpayer bailouts, but provided very little back to communities.

Resources wasted: Although the company had been losing market share, and revenues/profits were down, they had no specific method of measuring how much the overall devaluation of brands within the financial services sector had cost them.

Opportunity for a Solution: Key senior field leaders approached me and my co-author Alan Lysaght to do some form of community outreach program based on our international best-selling book, ABCs of Making Money for Teens. We created a workshop called "The ABCs of Talking to Your Kids About Money." We then trained hundreds of financial advisors on how to deliver our workshop. They in turn delivered hundreds of free workshops to parent groups across America. The program was very well received by parents and various community groups who hosted the workshop. The financial advisors received excellent free media attention, and as a result of the goodwill and service provided to the parents, they gained thousands of new clients (and many financial products were sold).

Financial investment required: Total cost for the program: around $800,000.

Improvement generated: Although the benefits to the company are all ongoing, one senior executive estimates profits linked to this program between $22 to $30 million.

Tracked ROI: 27.5:1.

Strategic Talent Management

TM Solution: Doubling the Potential Market Overnight

Case study: Small fashion retailer.
Problem/ Profit Opportunity: A high-end women's boutique owner asked me how to increase the percentage of sales.
Resources wasted: With the current level of sales, she was barely breaking even. Fixed costs per year were $185,000, including base pay for minimum staffing.
Opportunity for a Solution: A radical change was needed for dealing with the males who accompanied the women shoppers. In the past, the women were well catered to while the men were virtually ignored. The result was that the men felt uncomfortable in the shop and encouraged their wives/girlfriends to hurry up; so many sales opportunities were lost. The first thing was to train the fashion consultants to acknowledge the men and try to make them feel comfortable, and if possible engage in the shopping experience. An area in the middle of the shop was created with several comfortable chairs and magazines for men to occupy themselves. Hot coffee and tea were also offered to the men. The result was that the men became quite welcomed and comfortable to the point where the average length of visit by a couple increased from 4 minutes to 18. Sales consultants also created a file on each woman with key information; sizes, style preferences, etc., and discreetly handed the men a business card, so that if they ever wanted to surprise their partner, they could shop with the help of the consultant. This one idea alone created a huge boost in sales.
Financial investment required: Furniture, espresso machine: $7,000, training: $5,000. Total cost $12,000.
Improvement generated: Profits after first year of implementation: $71,500.
Tracked ROI: 6:1.

Strategic Talent Management

Chapter Six: Getting Started...Now!

Why you must start turning your TM into a profit center should be abundantly clear by this point.

Who should be involved in the process of converting TM into a bottom line driver? Everyone who is involved in making key Talent Management investments, starting from the CEO to all managers. Special emphasis must be placed on converting the traditional mindsets of formal TM practitioners.

When should this process start? Right now! The longer senior executives wait before demanding that TM be accountable for their investments and corresponding returns, the more money is shed from the bottom line.

Where should this change take place? It needs to start at the boardroom level and cascade down so that every department embraces the change.

How is the last piece. Throughout this book, I have provided many case examples of real-life clients I have helped using this system. I have included many practical ready-to-use tools, templates, and checklists to help you get started right away. This final section will offer some concluding thoughts to pull together the implementation of the concepts and best practices offered in this book.

TM-Driven Solutions Quick Reference Chart Developed by Michael Mercer

Problem: Low productivity

Possible Solutions	Ideas/Inspirations
Piecework pay	
Employee contests	
Suggestion system	
Interns and trainees	
Management bonuses	
Net gain sharing	
Merit pay	
Wellness program	

Strategic Talent Management

Possible Solutions	Ideas/Inspirations
Engagement surveys	
Team-building exercises	
Pre-selection assessment tools	
Reference checks	
Competency interviews	
Onboarding program	
Probationary period	
Training program	
Frequent feedback	
Positive discipline	

Problem: Employee turnover, absenteeism and tardiness

Possible Solutions	Ideas/Inspirations
Piecework pay	
Employee contests	
Merit pay	
Employer-supported child care	
Accident reduction program	
Exit interviews	
Probationary period	
Wellness program	
Engagement surveys	
Competency interviews	
Pre-selection assessment tools	
Reference checks	
Frequent feedback	
Positive discipline	

Strategic Talent Management

Problem: Insurance costs

Possible Solutions	Ideas/Inspirations
Wellness program	
Accident reduction program	
Pre-selection assessment tools	
Reference checks	
Competency interviews	
On-boarding program	
Positive discipline	
Frequent feedback	

Problem: Poor sales performance

Possible Solutions	Ideas/Inspirations
Commission structure	
Training program	
Pre-selection assessment tools	
Reference checks	
Competency interviews	
On-boarding program	
Positive discipline	
Frequent feedback	
Train non-sales support people to sell	

Making profitable HR a reality

Hopefully by now you feel you have ample ideas, tools, and templates to turn your HR function into a profit center. Here are six simple steps to help you with implementation.

1. Share and obtain buy-in of the "HR as a Profit Center" concept with your entire senior management and HR team.

2. Make use of "The PROFIT Model for Maximizing ROI in HR" to prepare a solid business case before making any major HR investments mandatory.

Strategic Talent Management

3. Properly support and resource HR investments.

4. Measure and hold people accountable for the ROI of investments made.

5. Share success stories throughout your organization to acknowledge the contributions made by the HR Profit center, while reinforcing the new mindset and behaviors. Methods of sharing the good news include: company newsletter, intranet site, presentations to managers and employees, one-on-one meetings, and CEO blogs.

6. Reward HR leaders for their contributions to the bottom line, as you would any other profit-generating executive.

I encourage you to keep referring back to this book, as it is a constant source of practical information. Be sure to take advantage of the many charts and questionnaires to ensure you fully benefit from turning HR into a profit center. Once you apply the principles covered in this book, the odds of being successful are in your favor.

Best of success!

Dr. Denis Cauvier

> **It is not necessary to change.**
> **Survival is not mandatory.**
>
> W. Edwards Deming

Strategic Talent Management

To connect with Dr. Cauvier:

- Website: www.deniscauvier.com
- Email: denis@deniscauvier.com
- LinkedIn: http://www.linkedin.com/denis-cauvier
- Twitter: @deniscauvier
- Phone: 613.864.7750

Dr. Denis Cauvier Seminars International is committed to providing its clients with customized solutions tailored to their unique requirements. Practical, results-oriented training, consulting, and professional speaking solutions are available in the following areas:

- Stop $pending money on your people: How to turn HR into a profit center
- How to engage your team and create strategic advantages during tough economic times
- Leading and engaging multi-generational teams
- How to attract and retain great people in today's labor market
- New horizons: the future of leadership development
- Delivering true customer-centric service
- Hired 2.0: Recruiting exceptional talent at the speed of light
- How to keep your staff productive and happy
- The F.A.C.T.S of Engaging and Retaining GREAT People

For more information about how Dr. Denis Cauvier Seminars International services can help your organization, please contact: denis@deniscauvier.com

www.ingramcontent.com/pod-product-compliance
Lightning Source LLC
Chambersburg PA
CBHW070407200326
41518CB00011B/2103